# Urban Consumer Theory

GEOFFREY K. TURNBULL

with commentary by
James R. Follain
and by
C. F. Sirmans

# URBAN CONSUMER THEORY

AREUEA Monograph Series, No. 2

THE URBAN INSTITUTE PRESS
Washington, D.C.

7-9-02

Library of Congress Cataloging in Publication Data

Turnbull, Geoffrey K.

   Urban Consumer Theory/Geoffrey K. Turnbull;
 with commentary by James R. Follain and C. F. Sirmans
1.  Consumer behavior.  2.  Sociology, urban.  3.  Urban
Economics.  4.  Real estate business.  I.  Title.  II.  Series.

HF5415.32.T94                    1995                    95-4833
333.33'8—dc20                                            CIP

ISBN 0-87766-645-8 (paper, alk. paper)
ISBN 0-87766-644-X (cloth, alk. paper)

Printed in the United States of America

Distributed by University Press of America

4720 Boston Way            3 Henrietta Street
Lanham, MD 20706           London   WC2E 8LU   ENGLAND

The Urban Institute Press is a refereed press. Its Editorial Advisory Board makes publication decisions on the basis of referee reports solicited from recognized experts in the field. Established and supported by the Urban Institute, the Press disseminates policy research on important social and economic problems, not only by Institute staff but also by outside authors.

*Urban Consumer Theory*, by Geoffrey K. Turnbull, is an AREUEA Monograph.

Conclusions are those of the authors and do not necessarily reflect the views of staff members, officers, trustees, advisory groups, or funders of The Urban Institute or The American Real Estate and Urban Economics Association.

# ACKNOWLEDGMENTS

I would like to thank Tony Yezer for his unfailing patience and help throughout the entire writing process. His prodding helped remove rough edges and his judgment and guidance were crucial for keeping the manuscript within manageable proportions. I am also grateful to the students who worked through earlier versions of this monograph. Their experiences helped shape the ultimate content and presentation. Finally, I owe a special thanks to my wife, Carolyn, whose unwavering support never ceases to amaze me.

# CONTENTS

**Tables**

**Figures**

# FOREWORD

The Urban Institute's commitment to studying urban problems and strategies to alleviate them is reflected in the central role urban economists have always played in the Institute's own work. Duncan MacRae, Robert Buckley, and James Follain are all Institute alumni. George Peterson and Raymond Struyk are among the urban economists currently on staff.

The importance we attach to urban economics (including real estate economics) as an analytic lens for studying the city's characteristics and problems, and the impacts of public policy on them, makes the Institute a most appropriate publisher for the Monograph Series sponsored by the American Real Estate and Urban Economics Association (AREUEA).

The intent of the AREUEA series is to summarize and synthesize recent research developments in an easily accessible form—for use by teachers, students, and practitioners (including urban planners, real estate investors, appraisers, the housing policy community, home and commercial builders, and the real estate finance industry).

This second book in the AREUEA monograph series makes two major contributions to the literature on urban consumer theory—the theory of the spatial dimension of household work-residence location decisions. First, it brings together the many separate pieces of theoretical work that now exist into a comprehensive, unified framework. This is an important addition to the field because the incentive structure underlying consumer decisions to change locations underlies housing markets and land-use theory, as well as the economic dynamics of cities and city systems.

The second contribution of the book is to connect up, for the first time, the predictions of household relocation theory with the policy world. This includes the whole range of programs that supplement the income of poor and near-poor households and/or subsidize their housing, as well as the myriad of regulations affecting land markets.

The whole debate over demand- versus supply-side incentives in the housing market is a major part of the policy context.

I expect this book to be helpful for many years to come to the teachers, students, and practitioners for whom it is written, as well as to the wider policy community.

William Gorham
President

# Chapter One

# A UNIFIED APPROACH TO
# URBAN CONSUMER THEORY

Over the last 30 years, urban economics has established itself as a distinct field in economics. Real estate economics and urban economics have both evolved beyond being minor extensions of standard neoclassical microtheory to develop a common core of theories. Whereas standard neoclassical microtheory typically assumes a nonspatial economy in which all economic activities occur at a single point in space, the distinctive feature of real estate and urban economics is the formal treatment of spatial economic relations. The core urban and real estate economic theories have been developed to study how spatial economic relations are driven by the need to transport goods and services or consumers between various locations.

Consumer location theory focuses on the spatial dimension of household work-residence decisions, and as such, provides the microfoundation for much of urban and real estate economics. This book provides a complete exposition of consumer location theory, or what is more commonly called urban consumer theory. By bringing together various models scattered throughout the literature into one comprehensive, unified framework, I emphasize the parallels between the development of nonspatial and spatial consumer theories, which can be exploited to simplify location demand analysis. I demonstrate, for example, how the introduction of location choice offers the consumer another margin for adjustment to economic changes, in addition to the traditional margin of quantity consumed. By articulating the theoretical connections between location demand theory and traditional nonspatial demand theory, I describe how the consumer response to economic changes includes systematic feedback effects of location demand into goods demands to either reinforce or offset the direct or nonlocational effects of parameter changes on goods demands. The traditional comparative static properties of goods demands are therefore systematically altered by the introduction of spatial considerations.[1]

The urban consumer theory literature has reached a stage at which interested readers can benefit from a unified survey of method, techniques, and results. This study provides such a review incorporating diverse sources and presenting results in a single, integrated framework. By presenting rigorous complete mathematical as well as intuitive and graphical derivations of all important results, this volume functions both as a textbook and as a handbook serving a wide range of interested readers in urban economics and real estate economics.

---

## 1.1 WHY PARTIAL EQUILIBRIUM THEORY?

Urban consumer theory, as the name indicates, is partial equilibrium analysis. The focus is the single consumer choosing consumption of goods, housing services, and where to reside and/or to work. There are several reasons for maintaining a narrow focus on partial equilibrium theory. First, partial equilibrium theory is the microfoundation for market-level and aggregate models, and so must be considered in detail in any event. Second, some of the complications studied in the partial equilibrium literature, like location demand under uncertainty, are not fully developed in the market-level and general equilibrium literatures. Third, pedagogy is enhanced by a unified treatment of all topics without the further complications of aggregation.[2] The partial equilibrium approach taken here lends itself to clear demonstrations of how comparative statics hinge upon economically intuitive relations easily recognized from standard nonspatial demand theory.

The goal of this study is to present a unified treatment of urban consumer theory. Interestingly, standard intermediate and first-semester graduate microeconomics courses typically spend up to one-third of course time dealing with consumer theory. The justification for prominent treatment is well established: the theory of the individual consumer underlies the theories of market demand and markets, and insight into the latter theories requires knowledge of the former. Real estate and urban economists, however, rarely have the same luxury. Field theory courses often cursorily treat consumer location demand per se and, instead, almost immediately delve into aggregate consumer behavior at the market level. Focusing on bid rent functions for groups of consumer types reinforces the focus on aggregate relations and makes it more difficult to draw upon the logical connections between nonspatial consumer theory and spatial consumer theory.[3]

Still, whether explicitly or implicitly, urban consumer theory underlies housing markets and land-use theories developed for use in urban and real estate economics. Its role in residential land-use theory is more explicit than in other applications, given the treatment of the microfoundation in the original models developed by Alonso (1964) and Muth (1969), in particular.[4] The theory also underlies various extensions of land-use models—for example, dealing with the spatial impact of transportation systems,[5] location-specific amenities and neighborhood externalities, as well as spatial segregation of consumers by income, race, or other characteristics.[6] The theory also provides the microfoundation for housing markets simulation models with or without explicit spatial components (Kain 1987).

Less obvious, but still crucial, is the role of urban consumer theory in the aggregate urban economics models of systems of cities. To keep the analysis tractable, the systems-of-cities approach uses aggregate analysis, which suppresses intraurban area spatial equilibrium. Although there is no explicit consideration of intraurban spatial dimension, the models nonetheless implicitly assume intraurban spatial equilibrium throughout.[7] More explicit use of consumer location equilibrium conditions or derived bid rent functions for land appear in the dynamic models of urban growth and the residential land development process.[8] Urban consumer theory clearly serves as the foundation for this line of literature as well.

In summary, urban consumer theory provides the microfoundation for a wide range of market and aggregate models. That by itself is reason enough to warrant this study's close attention. But just as important is the predictive content of the partial equilibrium theory itself, providing a simple model that yields rich predictions about urban spatial structure.[9]

---

### 1.2 OUTLINE OF THIS VOLUME

Each chapter of this volume is subdivided by topic and organized for easy reference, allowing the reader to skip chapters or sections without loss of continuity, as well as to cross-reference between chapters where results or derivations interrelate.

The general outline of the remainder of this monograph is as follows. Chapter 2 provides a thorough analysis of the urban consumer model and systematically presents its major variants and extensions. The chapter derives and explains established predictions of the theory for monocentric markets: a decreasing and convex housing price function with respect to distance from the central business district (CBD), increasing housing demand with distance, decreasing noncentral employment wages with distance from the CBD, as well as complete comparative static analyses of housing and location demands and labor/leisure choice. Chapter 3 demonstrates how the models can be applied to partial equilibrium analysis of public-sector institutions, examining how taxes, public services, and housing subsidies affect location and housing demands.

The study then turns to recent extensions of location demand theory into spatial uncertainty analysis, providing a comprehensive synthesis of the new literature on this topic. Chapter 4 summarizes uncertainty theory in the nonspatial context, explaining theoretical tools needed for subsequent spatial analysis. Chapter 5 examines housing and location demands under uncertainty. Two types of investigation are provided in this chapter: formal analysis and the less-formal graphical approach (the latter of which has been neglected in the literature). And in keeping with the overall theme of this presentation, the uncertainty analysis is tied to both the certainty spatial analysis and the nonspatial uncertainty theory of consumer behavior.

Chapter 6 presents brief concluding remarks. Two commentaries on the main text then follow, the first by James R. Follain and the second by C. F. Sirmans.

---

**Notes**

1. Further, the known properties of nonspatial goods demands, homogeneity, negative compensated own-price effects, symmetric compensated cross-price effects, and the Slutsky equation identifying compensated price and income effects need to be modified in the spatial case (Turnbull 1993c, 1994).

2. Not only must market-level aggregation address the different equilibria with and without the effects of intercity migration but also the effects of assuming absentee landowners (wherein all land rents escape the otherwise closed model) or resident landowners (wherein all land rents accrue to the resident population in some form or another). See, for example, Wheaton (1974) for the open versus closed migration models with absentee landowners and Pines and Sadka (1986) and Sasaki (1987) for models with resident landowners.

3. See Straszheim (1987) for an excellent survey of consumer land-use theory using the bid rent approach. Wheaton (1977a) explained why the bid rent approach and the approach taken in this monograph are equivalent.

4. For the monocentric residential land-use theory, see Wheaton (1974), Miyao (1975), Hartwick et al. (1976), Polinsky and Rubinfeld (1978), Pines and Sadka (1986), Sasaki

(1987), and Pasha (1992). Mills (1967) and Muth (1969) explicitly introduced housing demand in their land-use theory. Brueckner (1987) provided a synthesis of the single-consumer-type models. See White (1976), Weiland (1987), Yinger (1992b), and Turnbull (1993b) for models of land use in polycentric cities.

5. Solow and Vickery (1971) and Mills and de Ferranti (1971) are two classic references.

6. See Rose-Ackerman (1975), Courant and Yinger (1977), Kern (1981), and Yinger (1976, 1992a) for analyses of endogenous segregation by race, and Wheaton (1977b), Anas and Kim (1992), and chapter 2, this volume, for endogenous segregation by income.

7. See Henderson (1974, 1982) and Upton (1981) for complete treatments.

8. See Ohls and Pines (1975), Miyao (1977), Anas (1978), Fujita (1982), Wheaton (1982), Turnbull (1988a, b), and Helsley and Sullivan (1991).

9. See Muth (1985) for commentary on this point. In addition to the evidence summarized in chapters 2 and 5, see also Hamilton (1982), Brueckner and Fansler (1983), Bender and Hwang (1985), Blackley and Follain (1987), White (1988), Cropper and Gordon (1991), Thurston and Yezer (1991), Herrin and Kern (1992), McMillen, Jarmin, and Thorsnes (1992), and Small and Song (1992) for empirical tests of various implications of the theory and its simplest aggregate versions.

# Chapter Two

# HOUSING AND LOCATION CHOICE

The consumer models developed by Alonso (1964: 18–35) and Muth (1969: 17–36) represent seminal, complete statements of modern residential location demand theory, providing the logical foundation for spatial models of urban land-use patterns.[1] Recognizing this important role, the papers by Brown (1985), DeSalvo (1977a, b, 1985), and Mankin (1972) provided rigorous analyses of the basic monocentric consumer model and its implications, along with various extensions to study the implications of noncentralized employment and endogenous leisure choice. This chapter presents the partial equilibrium theory of urban household behavior under certainty. The discussion begins with the simplest formulation, the monocentric completely centralized employment model attributable to Muth. Each subsequent section introduces different complicating factors to the basic model, spanning the development of the literature: leisure choice (section 2.2), local or non-CBD employment (section 2.3), and local employment and leisure choice (section 2.4). The conclusion appears in section 2.5.

## 2.1 THE BASIC MODEL

The monocentric urban area is situated on a featureless plane, centered on the central business district (CBD), a dimensionless point at which all employment and shopping activities take place. Consider a household, traveling regularly to the CBD to work and shop, choosing consumption and residence location to maximize utility subject to a budget constraint. Radial transportation routes are ubiquitous, so that the household's transportation costs per period, $T$, are an increasing function of the distance between residence location and the CBD. Ordinarily, $T$ is also a function of household wage income to capture the value of time spent commuting as well as out-of-pocket money costs of commuting (Muth 1969; DeSalvo 1977b): $T(k, I)$, where $k$ is the commuting distance, which also serves as the index of residence location, and $I$ is household wage income. By assumption, $\partial T/\partial k = T_k > 0$, $T_{kk} \leq 0$, $0 < T_I < 1$ (so that greater gross income yields greater net income after transportation costs incurred), and $T_{kI} > 0$ (so that greater wage income increases the value of time spent commuting, which increases the marginal travel costs of distance). A simpler form, $T(k)$, appears in the literature as well; see, for example, the certainty model of aggregate land use in Wheaton (1974) and the uncertainty theory approaches studied in chapter 5.

Adopting Muth's approach of excluding distance from the utility function (DeSalvo 1977b), the household's problem is

$$\max_{x,y,k} U(x, y) \text{ subject to } I = P(k)x + y + T(k, I), \quad (2.1)$$

where $x$ = housing consumption, $y$ = nonhousing consumption, $I$ = household gross income per period, and $P(k)$ = housing rental price. The price of nonhousing consumption is normalized to one without loss of generality, but the housing price function $P(k)$ is unspecified at the outset. The characteristics of $P(k)$ are deduced as implications of location equilibrium in the following analysis.

Before proceeding to the analysis itself, it should be noted that this study adopts the convention of defining the demands derived from utility maximization subject to a budget constraint as "Marshallian" and the demands derived from expenditure minimization subject to a utility constraint as "Hicksian." It is important for what follows to remember that the Marshallian and Hicksian terminology refer only to the standard consumer choice paradigm, that is, the usual consumer choice theory holding location unchanged.

The properties of traditional Marshallian demand functions determine the location choice model predictions. To begin, define implicit Marshallian demand functions for housing and the composite good for the household located at a given location $k$ as

$$[x(P, I^0), y(P, I^0)] \equiv \text{argmax } [U(x, y) \text{ s.t. } I^0 = Px + y], \quad (2.2)$$

where $P = P(k)$ and $I^0 = I - T(k, I)$. Household demand for housing and nonhousing consumption at location, $k$, satisfies the usual marginal rate of substitution equals price ratio condition ($MRS_{x,y} = P$) and can be graphically depicted (as in figure 2.1) as the tangency between indifference curve $U^1$ and the budget constraint facing the consumer at distance $k$.

Given the optimal consumption at each location defined by equation (2.2), the household's problem is to select the appropriate loca-

Figure 2.1 LOCATION CHOICE

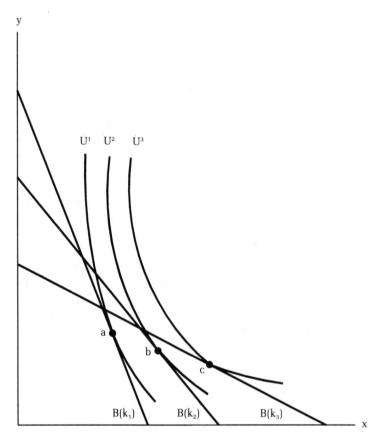

tion. Net income $I - T(k, I)$ and housing price $P(k)$ vary by location, so that the budget line depicted in figure 2.1 shifts and rotates as $k$ changes. To illustrate, denote the location-specific budget line $y = I - T(k, I) - P(k)x$ by $B(k)$. The vertical intercept of the budget line $B(k)$ shifts downward for larger $k$ because net income declines as travel cost rises [$T(k_1, I) < T(k_2, I)$ for $k_1 < k_2$ in the figure]. The budget line $B(k)$ also rotates shallower for larger $k$ because housing price declines with greater distance (as shown later).

Graphically, the household selects location in this model by choosing $k$ (hence the budget constraint), leaving the household on the highest indifference curve when compared to all curves tangent to their respective location-specific budget constraints. Denote the maximum utility obtainable from $B(k_j)$ as $U^j$. The location choice problem for the household is depicted in figure 2.1 as selecting the $k$, hence $B(k)$, that reaches the highest indifference curve, $U^3$ in figure 2.1.

Mathematically, the location-choice problem is solved by substituting problem (2.2) into $U(x, y)$ to obtain the indirect utility function

$$V[P(k), I - T(k, I)] \equiv U[x(P, I^0), y(P, I^0)], \qquad (2.3)$$

Formulated this way, (2.2) gives the household's optimal consumption at any given location $k$, corresponding to points $a$, $b$, and $c$ in figure 2.1. To find the optimal location (and by [2.2] the optimal consumption at this location), the household's problem is

$$\max_k V[P(k), I - T(k, I)]. \qquad (2.4)$$

Taken together, problems (2.2) and (2.4) are equivalent to (2.1). The household's optimal $k$ satisfies the location equilibrium condition $dV/dk = V_k = 0$, which, upon total differentiation of (2.3), gives

$$V_P P_k - V_I T_k = 0. \qquad (2.5)$$

This condition requires that the consumer reside where the marginal utility of changing housing price equals the marginal utility of changing travel costs. Appendix A demonstrates the well-known properties of $V$ for this model: $V_P = -\lambda x(P, I^0)$ and $V_I = \lambda$, where $\lambda$ (the marginal utility of income) is the Lagrangian multiplier from the constrained optimization problem (2.2). Because $\lambda > 0$ (see appendix A), equation (2.5) reduces to the following condition, known in the literature as "Muth's equation,"

$$-P_k x(P, I^0) - T_k = 0, \qquad (2.6)$$

or $P_k = -T_k/x$. Muth's equation can, in principle, be solved for the optimal location $k^*$. I defer interpreting this important equation until after some key intermediate results are derived.

Substituting $k^*$ into the implicit Marshallian demand function (2.2) yields the optimal housing consumption at $k^*$ as

$$x^* = x[P(k^*), I - T(k^*, I)] \qquad (2.7)$$

and similarly for $y^*$. Equation (2.6) and function (2.7) represent the key relationships used in the analysis to follow.

**Housing Price Function**

The spatial characteristics of $P(k)$ easily follow from (2.6): *Housing price is a decreasing strictly convex function of distance from the CBD* (i.e., $P_k < 0$, $P_{kk} > 0$). Use (2.6) to show $P_k = -T_k/x < 0$, since

$T_k > 0$. The second-order condition to (2.4) is used to show the convexity result, $P_{kk} > 0$. To do so, note that the second-order condition (SOC) is $V_{kk} < 0$. Differentiating Muth's equation (2.6) with respect to $k$, the SOC $V_{kk} < 0$ for indirect utility to be maximized at $k^*$ requires that the second derivative of the left-hand side of (2.6) be negative:[2]

$$D = -P_{kk}x - T_{kk} - P_k[(\partial x/\partial P)P_k - (\partial x/\partial I^0)T_k] < 0. \qquad (2.8)$$

From Muth's equation (2.6), $T_k = -P_k x$, so that substituting into the expression in brackets yields

$[(\partial x/\partial P)P_k - (\partial x/\partial I^0)T_k]$

$$= P_k[\partial x/\partial P + x(P, I^0)(\partial x/\partial I^0)] = P_k(\partial X/\partial P) > 0, \qquad (2.9)$$

where $X(P, U^*)$ is the compensated or Hicksian housing demand at $U^* = V[P(k^*), I - T(k^*, I)]$. From the Slutsky equation it is known that the total Marshallian price effect is the sum of substitution and income effects, or $\partial x/\partial P = \partial X/\partial P - x(\partial x/\partial I^0)$, which allows the substitution of the Hicksian term $\partial X/\partial P$ for $\partial x/\partial P + x(\partial x/\partial I^0)$, and yields the second equality above. The sign of (2.9) follows from $P_k < 0$ and the negative pure substitution effect of a change in housing price on housing demand. Using $P_k < 0$, $T_{kk} \leq 0$, and (2.9), $P_{kk} > 0$ must hold in order for (2.8) to hold. Therefore, $P(k)$ is strictly convex in distance, as asserted.

By differentiating Marshallian demand for housing (2.2) with respect to $k$, using $P(k)$ and $I^0 = I - T(k, I)$, the spatial variation in housing demand, the housing demand gradient, is found to be

$$\partial x/\partial k = (\partial x/\partial P)P_k - (\partial x/\partial I^0)T_k = P_k(\partial X/\partial P) > 0, \qquad (2.10)$$

where the second equality follows from (2.9). Thus, *housing demand increases with distance*, as pictured in the left-hand panel of figure 2.2, and the optimal housing consumption is $x^*$, the demand at optimal location $k^*$.

Muth's equation (2.6) can now be interpreted using figure 2.2. The marginal cost of distance (MCD) is the increase in commuting costs incurred by residing farther away from the CBD, or MCD $= T_k$. Given that housing price declines with greater distance, $-P_k x$ measures the marginal benefit of distance (MBD) as the savings on housing expenditures obtainable by moving farther away from the CBD. Muth's equation therefore maintains location equilibrium where MBD $=$ MCD. The SOC $V_{kk} < 0$ requires dMBD/dk $<$ dMCD/dk or that MBD cut MCD from above, as depicted in figure 2.2.

Figure 2.2  HOUSEHOLD EQUILIBRIUM LOCATION AND HOUSING DEMAND
(where MCD is drawn for $T_{kk} < 0$ case)

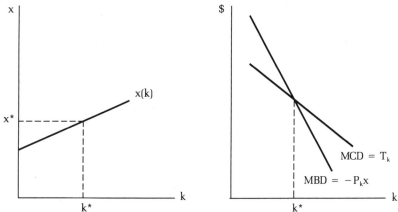

Notes: MDB, marginal benefit of distance; MCD, marginal cost of distance.

## Comparative Statics

Muth's equation is the location equilibrium condition and plays a key
role in deriving comparative static predictions from this model.[3] Consider a shift parameter, $\alpha$, which alters income, transportation costs,
the housing price function, or household preferences. The complete
comparative static predictions and their relation with traditional nonspatial demand theory are derived for the general case, as follows.
The effect of a change in $\alpha$ on $k^*$, $dk^*/d\alpha$, is found by implicitly
differentiating (2.6). Using (2.7), the effect of $\alpha$ on housing consumption is

$$dx^*/d\alpha = (\partial x/\partial\alpha) + (\partial x/\partial k)(dk^*/d\alpha).$$

The first right-hand-side term is the direct effect of $\alpha$ on housing
demand, holding location unchanged. The second term is the indirect
effect of $\alpha$ on housing demand: $\alpha$ affects the optimal location; the
change in optimal location in turn alters the household's optimal
housing consumption. The total effect of $\alpha$ on housing demand therefore comprises a direct effect (the first term) and an indirect or "location" effect (the second term).

Equation (2.10) is used to rewrite the preceding equation as

$$dx^*/d\alpha = (\partial x/\partial\alpha) + P_k(\partial X/\partial P)(dk^*/d\alpha). \tag{2.11}$$

Looking at (2.11), it is apparent that the total effect of parameter $\alpha$ on
$x^*$ is determined by the comparative static properties of nonspatial

housing demand (specifically $\partial x/\partial \alpha$ and $\partial X/\partial P$) and $dk^*/d\alpha$. The detailed cases below demonstrate that $dk^*/d\alpha$ is determined entirely by the properties of nonspatial housing demand.[4]

## HOUSING PRICE CHANGES

Introduce the shift parameter $\alpha$ into the price function, $P(k, \alpha)$. There are three types of changes associated with a price "increase," $P_\alpha > 0$. The upward displacement entails a vertical parallel shift ($P_{k\alpha} = 0$) or a vertical shift combined with some rotation that leaves the price surface flatter ($P_{k\alpha} > 0$) or steeper ($P_{k\alpha} < 0$).

Implicitly differentiating Muth's equation (2.6) yields[5]

$$dk^*/d\alpha = [P_{k\alpha}x(P, I^0) + P_k P_\alpha(\partial x/\partial P)]\lambda/V_{kk}, \qquad (2.12)$$

while differentiating spatial housing demand (2.7) with respect to $\alpha$ reveals

$$dx^*/d\alpha = (\partial x/\partial P)P_\alpha + P_k(\partial X/\partial P)(dk^*/d\alpha). \qquad (2.13)$$

Recalling that $\lambda > 0$, $V_{kk} < 0$, and assuming $\partial x/\partial P < 0$, $P_{k\alpha} \geq 0$ is sufficient for $dk^*/d\alpha < 0$ in (2.12), hence $dx^*/d\alpha < 0$ in (2.13). *Housing demand falls and the household's optimal commute distance falls in response to an upward shift in the housing price function, whether parallel or coupled with a shallower slope. The consumer's response to a steeper housing price function slope is ambiguous.*

Intuitively, the upward shift ($P_\alpha > 0$) and counterclockwise rotation ($P_{k\alpha} > 0$) in the price function both decrease the MBD in figure 2.3,

Figure 2.3  INCREASE IN HOUSING PRICE WITH $P_{k\alpha} > 0$

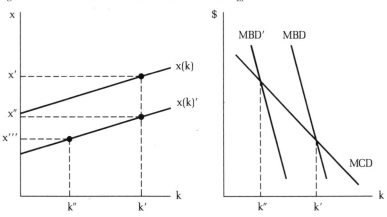

Notes: MDB, marginal benefit of distance; MCD, marginal cost of distance.

shifting the curve in that figure downward and leading to a more central optimal location for the household. The more central location by itself stifles housing demand (the second term, location effect, in [2.13]), reinforcing the direct effect of higher housing price on demand at each location (the first term in [2.13]). As is clear from figure 2.3, the direct effect of a housing price shift on housing demand is x′ to x″, induced by the shift in the housing consumption gradient. The location effect, on the other hand, is x″ to x″′, induced by the movement along the new (lower) gradient.

If, on the other hand, the price function becomes steeper ($P_{k\alpha} < 0$) as it shifts upwards, then the steeper gradient by itself increases the rate of savings on housing expenditures from moving farther out, increasing MBD. The upward shift in $P(k)$, of course, decreases housing demand at each k, thus reducing MBD. The net effect on household location is ambiguous in this case, as the $P_{k\alpha} < 0$ effect on MBD tends to offset that of $P_\alpha > 0$.[6] Although it may seem unlikely, we cannot rule out the possibility that the steeper housing price gradient effect on MBD is sufficiently strong to yield a net increase in MBD, so that the household increases commuting distance, thereby providing a location effect on housing demand that offsets the direct effect of the higher housing price.

TRANSPORTATION COST CHANGES

Specify $T(k, I, \alpha)$, where $T_\alpha > 0$. From (2.6),

$$dk^*/d\alpha = [-P_k(\partial x/\partial I^0)T_\alpha + T_{k\alpha}]\lambda/V_{kk}. \qquad (2.14)$$

Recalling that $\lambda > 0$, $V_{kk} < 0$, $P_k < 0$, and $\partial x/\partial I^0 > 0$, clearly, $T_{k\alpha} \geq 0$ is sufficient for $dk^*/d\alpha < 0$ when x is a normal good, so that (2.11) yields

$$dx^*/d\alpha = -T_\alpha(\partial x/\partial I^0) + P_k(\partial X/\partial P)(dk^*/d\alpha) \qquad (2.15)$$

and $dx^*/\alpha < 0$ as well: *the consumer's optimal commuting distance and housing demand both fall in response to greater fixed or marginal transportation costs.*

The intuition behind this result differs somewhat from the price change case. By itself, an increase in travel costs ($T_\alpha > 0$) reduces net income, thereby reducing housing demand at each location and diminishing the MBD. If there were no change in the marginal cost of distance (that is, $T_{k\alpha} = 0$), then the reduction in MBD would prod the consumer to move closer to the CBD. The location effect of $T_\alpha > 0$

reinforces the direct effect of (2.15) so that the household's housing demand would decline as well.

If marginal transportation costs also rise ($T_{k\alpha} > 0$), then the MCD shifts upwards in figure 2.1, reinforcing the higher transportation cost effect on location choice. In this case, too, the location effect in (2.15) reinforces the direct effect in reducing housing demand. If, on the other hand, marginal transportation costs fall ($T_{k\alpha} < 0$), then the MCD shifts downwards in figure 2.3—which by itself tends to offset the effect of higher total transportation costs on the consumer's choice of location. Only if the downward shift in the MCD is sufficiently strong to completely offset the downward shift in MBD will the consumer actually increase $k^*$. And only in this case will the location effect of travel cost increases offset the direct effect of lower net income on housing demand in (2.15).

### TASTE CHANGES

Introduce a taste parameter $\alpha$ into $x(P, I^0, \alpha)$ such that $\partial x/\partial \alpha > 0$ signifies stronger tastes for housing per se. (Concomitant is $\partial y/\partial \alpha < 0$, of course.)[7] Following the general procedure above, the effect of stronger housing tastes on location and housing demand is equated as

$$dk^*/d\alpha = P_k(\partial x/\partial \alpha)\lambda/V_{kk} > 0 \qquad (2.16)$$

$$dx^*/d\alpha = \partial x/\partial \alpha + P_k^2(\partial x/\partial \alpha)(\partial X/\partial P)\lambda/V_{kk} > 0. \qquad (2.17)$$

This case is particularly easy to see. The stronger taste for housing increases the MBD at all $k$. This upward shift in MBD in figure 2.2 results in the household residing farther out ($dk^*/d\alpha > 0$). The stronger taste for housing, by itself, induces the household to increase housing demand (the upward shift in $x[k]$ in the figure or first term in [2.17]), while the incentive to move farther out (the locational effect) reinforces this direct effect (the movement along the higher $x[k]'$ surface in the figure, or the second term in [2.17]). As expected, the result is that *consumers with stronger tastes for housing relative to non-housing consumption will live farther away from the CBD to consume at locations where housing prices are lower.*

### INCOME CHANGES

To investigate the effects of income changes, specify $I = \alpha$. Proceeding as before, differentiate (2.6) to get

$$dk^*/d\alpha = P_k(\partial x/\partial I^0)(1 - T_I)\lambda/V_{kk} + T_{kI}\lambda/V_{kk}, \qquad (2.18)$$

and (2.7) yields

$$dx^*/d\alpha = (\partial x/\partial I^0)(1 - T_I) + P_k(\partial X/\partial P)(dk^*/d\alpha). \qquad (2.19)$$

If changes in income do not affect the marginal cost of distance—for example, as when nonwage income changes—then $T_{kI} = 0$ and the location effect always reinforces the direct effect of a change in income. If housing is a normal good when holding location unchanged, then $dk^*/d\alpha > 0$ and $dx^*/d\alpha > 0$ in this situation.

Increases in wage income, on the other hand, also increase the value of time spent commuting, so that $T_{k\alpha} > 0$. In light of (2.18) and (2.19), the assumption that Marshallian housing demand is a normal good is no longer sufficient to sign the wage income comparative statics. Because net income increases with $I$, $1 - T_I > 0$, and Marshallian normality ensures that the MBD increases with income, shifting the MBD curve upward in figure 2.2. This by itself increases the optimal distance, as revealed by the first term in (2.18). The increase in time cost of travel, however, shifts the MCD curve upward in the figure, which by itself decreases the optimal distance, as revealed by the second term in (2.18). The net effect of higher wage income on location therefore depends upon the relative shifts in these curves.

The wage income effect on location demand can be shown to hinge upon the relative sizes of housing demand and marginal transportation cost income elasticities. To see this, note that $\lambda/V_{kk} < 0$, so that (2.18) yields

$$dk^*/d\alpha = [P_k(\partial x/\partial I^0)(1 - T_I) + T_{kI}]\lambda/V_{kk} \gtreqless 0, \qquad (2.20)$$

as

$$-P_k(\partial x/\partial I^0)(1 - T_I) \gtreqless T_{kI}. \qquad (2.21)$$

From Muth's equation $-P_k = T_k/x$; substituting this into (2.21), the LHS becomes $T_k(\partial x/\partial I^0)(1 - T_I)/x$, so that multiplying both sides of (2.21) by $(I/T_k)$ reveals that (2.20) holds as

$$(\partial x/\partial I^0)(1 - T_I)I/x \gtreqless T_{kI}I/T_k. \qquad (2.22)$$

Since $dI^0/dI = (1 - T_I)$, one obtains $\partial x/\partial I = (\partial x/\partial I^0)(1 - T_I)$, so that (2.22) can be rewritten as

$$E(x, I) \gtreqless E(T_k, I), \qquad (2.23)$$

where $E(x, I)$ is the income elasticity of Marshallian housing demand and $E(T_k, I)$ is the income elasticity of the marginal cost of distance. So long as the former exceeds the latter, increases in wage income will increase the optimal distance, and the location effect of income in (2.19) will reinforce the direct effect.

The empirical evaluation of inequality (2.23) has been a source of controversy over the years. The first problem arises from the wide range of income elasticities for housing demand observed in the literature. To illustrate, deLeeuw's (1971) attempt to reconcile scattered income elasticity estimates implied a range from 0.8 to 1.0. Mayo (1981) reviewed subsequent empirical studies, leading him to conclude that "the permanent income elasticity of demand for housing is estimated to be well below one on average" (p. 112). Most estimates in his survey, though, were between 0.5 and 0.7, considerably below deLeeuw's range. What these surveys illustrate is the difficulty of pinning down a narrow range of values for the left-hand side of (2.23).

That the parameter itself may vary is a distinct possibility. Demonstrating this point is beyond the scope of this discussion, but it is interesting to note here that Goodman and Kawai (1986) concluded from their estimation that the income elasticity should be expected to vary across the range of household data and urban areas. Their "best" Box-Cox transformation estimates ranged from 0.6 to 1.0 over a two-standard-deviation interval centered on the means of their data. Note, coincidentally, that this range largely encompasses both deLeeuw's and Mayo's "reasonable" estimate ranges.

The other problem with evaluating (2.23) arises from the right-hand side, the income elasticity of MCD. Wheaton (1977b) used an income elasticity of housing demand equal to 0.7 and calculated an elasticity value of $E(T_k, I)$, which is close enough to the income elasticity of demand to conclude that $dk^*/dI = 0$, approximately; the urban consumer model provides no strong explanation of the positive income-distance relationship typical of U.S. cities.

Hekman (1980), however, offered two relevant points for consideration. First, he explained that including wage income in the travel cost function to capture the value of travel time violates the price normalization implicit in the inclusion of leisure in the composite commodity, $y$. Still, as the model with explicit leisure choice (section 2.2) illustrates, $dk^*/dI$ hinges upon an inequality like (2.23), even when the theoretically preferable treatment of commuting time is used.

Hekman's (1980) second argument again foreshadows the analysis of section 2.2. He argued that Wheaton's $E(T_k, I)$ calculation in (2.23) is itself deficient, since it does not account for the effects of secondary worker labor supply in the family. Hekman's insight is that since secondary workers' propensity to supply labor declines as primary worker income rises, $E(T_k', I)$ must be adjusted downward to take into account the *reduction* in household commuting time induced by the reduction in commuting (number of work trips) by the secondary worker as household income rises. Appropriately adjusting Wheaton's estimate leaves (2.23) with strictly greater than inequality: $dk^*/dI >$ 0, and the model explains the income-location pattern observed.

Further analysis is provided by DeSalvo (1985: 171–73), who used the leisure choice model of section 2.2 to show how virtually any income-location result can be forthcoming given the wide range of "reasonable" parameter estimates for both sides of (2.23). Nonetheless, Muth (1985) presented a straightforward conclusion to the matter: because the value of labor time is roughly one-half of total incremental travel costs, $E(T_k, I) = 0.5$ approximately, which yields $dk^*/dI > 0$ for virtually any reasonable value of the income elasticity estimates available.

In sum, the urban consumer theory does not provide an unequivocal prediction of the income-location pattern observed for households in U.S. cities, given the sensitivity of the predicted income-location effect to the range of parameter estimates available in the empirical literature. Still, the income-location explanatory power of the theory ranges from Wheaton's weak support to Muth's much stronger positive conclusion. In any case, the model clearly does not predict a location pattern contrary to what is observed.

## 2.2 LEISURE CHOICE

In the preceding model the consumer does not explicitly choose the amount of time he or she wishes to provide as labor, enjoy as leisure, or spend commuting. Given that additional travel requires additional time, the household's allocation of time to commuting varies with the choice of commuting distance. The model does not, however, spell out the trade-offs faced by the household: is leisure time or work time reduced or a combination of both?

DeSalvo (1985) extended the partial equilibrium location demand model to examine how labor-leisure-commute time choices alter the theoretical conclusions derived above. This section follows his analysis and then incorporates the effects of labor time rigidity required by a "standard" length workday. The labor time rigidity model allows one to demonstrate that the Alonso (1964) version of urban consumer theory can be viewed as a special case of the leisure choice generalization of Muth's model.

## The Model

This model retains earlier notation and assumptions, except for the following additions and changes. Define: $n$ = labor time, $z$ = leisure time, $t(k)$ = travel time (where additional travel takes more time, $t_k > 0$, and $t_{kk} \leq 0$), $w_0$ = nonlabor (lump-sum) income, and $w$ = wage rate. Given variable labor time, household income is now $I = w_0 + wn$. Commuters incur out-of-pocket expenses, $c(k)$, and travel time, $t(k)$. I assume $c_k > 0$ and $c_{kk} \leq 0$. The form of $T(k, I)$ becomes clear with additional model development.

Finally, available time is normalized to unity without loss of generality, so that

$$n + t + z = 1. \tag{2.24}$$

The variables $n$, $t$, and $z$ are therefore interpreted as the *proportions* of total time spent working, commuting, and in leisurely activity.

I assume that the household values additional leisure; household utility is $U(x, y, z)$, with $U_z > 0$. The household's problem is

$$\max_{x,y,z,n,k} U(x, y, z) \text{ s.t. } w_0 + wn = P(k)x + y + c(k) \tag{2.25}$$
$$n + t(k) + z = 1.$$

Notice that, given $t(k)$, travel time is chosen when the household determines distance.

Recasting the problem somewhat, solve the time constraint for labor time, $n = 1 - z - t(k)$. Substitute into the budget constraint to obtain

$$w_0 + w[1 - t(k)] - c(k) = P(k)x + y + wz. \tag{2.26}$$

The problem is now simplified by eliminating one constraint and the choice of $n$; problem (2.25) is now

$$\max_{x,y,z,k} U(x, y, z) \text{ s.t. } I^0 = P(k)x + y + wz, \tag{2.27}$$

where $I^0 = w_0 + w[1 - t(k)] - c(k)$ is now potential income available for nontravel activity, that is, consumption and leisure. In terms of the model without leisure choice, total potential income is now $w_0 + w$ and travel cost is $T = wt(k) + c(k)$. Notice $T_k = wt_k + c_k > 0$ and $T_{kk} = wt_{kk} + c_{kk} \leq 0$, while $T_w = t(k) > 0$ and $T_{wk} = t_k > 0$, with $1 > T_{wk} > 0$ because $t(k) < 1$. Total transportation costs therefore exhibit the same characteristics assumed for $T(k, I)$ in the earlier formulation.

The Marshallian demand at a given distance $k$ is defined as

$[x(P, w, I^0), y(P, w, I^0), z(P, w, I^0)]$

$$\equiv \text{argmax}[U(x, y, z) \text{ s.t. } I^0 = Px + y + wz]. \quad (2.28)$$

The first-order conditions (FOCs) for this problem are the usual conditions:[8] that money available for consumption at location $k$ be allocated among $x$, $y$, and $z$ such that all marginal rates of substitutions equal appropriate price ratios, where the "price" of leisure is the wage forgone by not working.

The price of housing and net income are both functions of distance in (2.28). Substituting (2.28) into $U(x, y, z)$ yields the indirect utility function:

$$V[P(k), w, I^0(k)] = U[x(P, w, I^0), y(P, w, I^0), z(P, w, I^0)]. \quad (2.29)$$

The optimal location $k^*$ is that which maximizes (2.29), the FOC for which implies Muth's equation, where $wt_k + c_k$ is the MCD:

$$-P_k x - wt_k - c_k = 0. \quad (2.30)$$

Introducing leisure choice into the model does not alter the location equilibrium condition; optimal location is still where the MBD, the savings on housing expenditures obtainable by moving toward a lower price, just equals the MCD, the additional travel cost.

## Housing Price Function

Equation (2.30) also demonstrates that the price function is negatively sloped over distance as an implication of equilibrium: $P_k = -(wt_k + c_k)/x < 0$. The SOC for location choice is $V_{kk} < 0$, which requires

$$-P_{kk}x - P_k(\partial x/\partial k) - wt_{kk} - c_{kk} < 0.$$

But $P_k < 0$, $\partial x/\partial k > 0$ by (2.31), and $wt_{kk} + c_{kk} \leq 0$ imply $P_{kk} > 0$: *The housing price function is decreasing convex in distance as in the model without leisure choice.*

The housing demand gradient is found by differentiating housing demand (2.28) with respect to distance:

$$\partial x/\partial k = (\partial x/\partial P)P_k - (\partial x/\partial I^0)(wt_k + c_k).$$

The Slutsky equation implies $\partial x/\partial P = \partial X/\partial P - x(\partial x/\partial I^0)$, so that the above becomes

$$\partial x/\partial k = (\partial X/\partial P)P_k + (\partial x/\partial I^0)[-P_k x - wt_k - c_k] \quad (2.31)$$

$$= (\partial X/\partial P)P_k > 0,$$

using Muth's equation ($-P_k x - wt_k - c_k = 0$) and the Substitution Theorem ($\partial X/\partial P < 0$) for the second equality. *Housing demand increases with distance when leisure is endogenous.*

Since leisure is variable in this model, the question arises: Is there a leisure gradient? Recalling that time can be spent only on leisure, work, or travel, and that travel increases with distance, this question is closely related to the existence of a labor-supply gradient over space.

To see how leisure demand varies with distance, differentiate Marshallian leisure demand (2.28) with respect to $k$ to find

$$\partial z/\partial k = (\partial z/\partial P)P_k - (\partial z/\partial I^0)[c_k + wt_k]. \qquad (2.32)$$

The Slutsky equation for cross-price effects is $\partial z/\partial P = \partial Z/\partial P - x(\partial z/\partial I^0)$, where $Z(P, w, U)$ is the Hicksian or compensated leisure demand. Substituting into the first RHS term in (2.32) obtains

$$\partial z/\partial k = (\partial Z/\partial P)P_k + (\partial z/\partial I^0)[-P_k x - wt_k - c_k].$$

The term in square brackets is zero by Muth's equation, so that

$$\partial z/\partial k = (\partial Z/\partial k)P_k \gtreqless 0, \text{ as } \partial Z/\partial P \gtreqless 0. \qquad (2.33)$$

This result has intuitive appeal. *Housing price falls and housing demand rises with distance, so that if leisure and housing are complements, then leisure increases with distance. When leisure and housing are substitutes, though, the household substitutes out of leisure and into more housing as the housing price falls with distance.*

Since labor supply is $n = 1 - t(k) - z(P, w, I^0)$, the labor supply gradient is determined by

$$dn/dk = -t_k - \partial z/\partial k. \qquad (2.34)$$

As known, $t_k > 0$; $\partial z/\partial k \geq 0$ is sufficient to establish a negatively inclined labor supply-distance relationship. *That is, for the complementary and unrelated goods cases, travel time increases and leisure increases or remains unchanged at greater distances: hence labor, the residual, must decline. This case yields the surprising result that those households working more hours consume less housing and live closer to the CBD than their leisure-consuming counterparts. Only when leisure and housing are strong enough substitutes to ensure that the reduction in leisure with distance exceeds the additional travel time will labor supply increase with distance in this model.*

### Comparative Statics with Endogenous Labor Supply

Proceeding as before, the shift parameter $\alpha$ is introduced into housing price and transportation cost functions to find the household's response to the change in these relations. The effects of tastes and wage and nonwage income on location and housing demand are also examined. The comparative statics are summarized in table 2.1.

### HOUSING PRICE CHANGES

Introduce $\alpha$ into the price function with $P_\alpha > 0$. The effect on location follows from (2.30) as

$$dk^*/d\alpha = [P_{k\alpha}x + P_k P_\alpha(\partial x/\partial P)]\lambda/V_{kk}. \qquad (2.35)$$

The first term in the numerator captures the price function rotation effect on MBD, while the second term captures the price function shift effect on MBD. The rotation to a steeper slope ($P_{k\alpha} \leq 0$) serves to reduce MBD, reinforcing the upward shift effect $P_\alpha > 0$, and leading to a reduction in distance, as in figure 2.3. Any tendency for a shallower slope, though, serves to offset the price shift effect. This is, of course, in accordance with earlier analysis.

Housing demand changes according to

$$dx^*/d\alpha = (\partial x/\partial P)P_\alpha + (\partial x/\partial k)(dk^*/d\alpha). \qquad (2.36)$$

The first term is the direct effect of price on demand, which is negative, whereas the second term is the location effect, which takes the sign of (2.35). As in the earlier case, the location effect may reinforce

Table 2.1  COMPARATIVE STATICS FOR CBD-EMPLOYED HOUSEHOLD

| Increase in: | Sufficient Conditions | Muth's Model | | Leisure Model | |
|---|---|---|---|---|---|
| | | $x^*$ | $k^*$ | $x^*$ | $k^*$ |
| Housing price | $P_{k\alpha} \geq 0$ | − | − | − | − |
| | $P_{k\alpha} < 0$ | ? | ? | ? | ? |
| Nonwage income | | + | + | + | + |
| Wage income | | ? | ? | ? | ? |
| | Consensus parameters | + | + or 0 | + | + or 0 |
| | Marshallian complements | | | ? | ? |
| | Unrelated | | | + | + or 0 |
| | Substitutes | | | + | + or 0 |
| Travel cost | $T_{k\alpha} \geq 0$ | − | − | − | − |
| | $T_{k\alpha} < 0$ | ? | ? | ? | ? |
| Housing tastes | | + | + | + | + |

Note: CBD, central business district.

or offset the direct effect on housing demand, depending upon the sign and strength of the price function rotation on $k^*$.

## TRANSPORTATION COST CHANGES

There are two types of transportation cost changes to consider: out-of-pocket and time costs. Interestingly, it turns out that each type of cost change has identical effects on housing and location demands. Further, the effects follow the simpler model case formally derived in the previous section: increases in travel cost, whether time or money, reduce net income and hence housing demand at each location, which in turn reduces the MBD in figure 2.1. At the same time, a steeper slope of $t(k)$ or $c(k)$ serves to increase MCD in figure 2.1, reinforcing the tendency of the lower MBD to reduce commute distance. Any flattening of $t(k)$ or $c(k)$ slopes, on the other hand, decreases MCD, offsetting the MBD effect on $k^*$. Finally, the direct effect of transportation cost changes on housing demand is negative, via the reduced net income effect, whereas the location effect on housing demand follows the effect on $k^*$.

## TASTE CHANGES

Here again, the results replicate the simpler model. Introduce $\alpha$ into housing demand such that $\partial x / \partial \alpha$ indicates a stronger taste for housing. The stronger taste for housing increases housing demand at each $k$, increasing the MBD. This increases $k^*$, which in turn reinforces the direct effect of $\alpha$ on housing demand. Unambiguously, housing demand increases with $\alpha$.[9]

## NONWAGE INCOME CHANGES

Because there is no distinction between wage and nonwage income in the earlier model, new results are anticipated. They include:

$$dk^*/dw_0 = P_k(\partial x/\partial I^0)\lambda/V_{kk} > 0 \text{ and} \qquad (2.37)$$

$$dx^*/dw_0 = (\partial x/\partial I^0) + (\partial x/\partial k)(dk^*/dw_0) > 0, \qquad (2.38)$$

using $I^0 = w_0 + w[1 - t(k)] - c(k)$. These results are remarkably simple. An increase in $w_0$ increases Marshallian housing demand, increasing MBD so that the household resides farther away from the CBD. Looking at (2.38), the direct effect of $w_0$ on housing demand is reinforced by the location effect, as the location farther out entails a move down the price gradient, the decrease in price prompting even greater housing demand.

WAGE CHANGES

Looking at wage changes, (2.39) resembles (2.18) when the substitutions $T_I = t(k)$ and $T_{kl} = t_k$ are made:

$$dk^*/dw = P_k(\partial x/\partial I^0)[1 - t(k)]\lambda/V_{kk} + t_k\lambda/V_{kk}. \qquad (2.39)$$

The location result here is therefore identical to the earlier result, and the empirical relation (2.23) in which the income elasticity of housing demand must exceed that of marginal transportation cost for $dk^*/dw > 0$ remains valid.

The effect of wage income on housing demand, on the other hand, is radically different from the earlier model. Differentiating (2.28) yields

$$dx^*/dw = (\partial x/\partial I^0)[1 - t(k)] + (\partial x/\partial w) + (\partial x/\partial k)(dk^*/dw). \qquad (2.40)$$

The direct effect of wage on housing demand now comprises the first two terms in (2.40). The first term captures the effect of the change in net potential income induced by the change in $w$. (Recall that some of the potential income is "spent," that is, forgone, by consuming leisure.) This effect is clearly positive, again recalling $t(k) < 1$. The second term in (2.40) captures the effect of the change in relative leisure/housing prices induced by a change in $w$. By definition, $\partial x/\partial w \geq 0$, as housing and leisure are Marshallian substitutes or complementary goods. Thus, if housing and leisure are substitutes or unrelated, the total direct effect of wage income on housing demand will be positive. On the other hand, if they are complements, the relative price effect tends to offset the net income effect on x, leaving the total direct effect ambiguous.

## Work Time Constraints

The preceding model assumes that the household can freely substitute between leisure, travel, and work. Consider now the implications of limiting time substitution for the household by restricting work time to a standard workday, N. The time constraint is now $N + t(k) + z = 1$, so that leisure is completely determined by the length of the household's commute:

$$z(k) = 1 - N - t(k). \qquad (2.41)$$

Substitute N and (2.41) into problem (2.27) to recast the equation as

$$\max_{x,k} U[x, I^0 - Px, 1 - N - t(k)], \qquad (2.42)$$

with $I^0 = w_0 + wN - c(k)$. Notice that distance now enters the utility function, as in Alonso's (1964) model. Thus, the result pointed out in Turnbull (1992b): Alonso's model can be viewed as a special case of the generalized Muth model of household behavior.

Marshallian housing demand is now conditional upon the level of leisure (which is parametric at each $k$):

$$x[P(k), I^0(k), z(k)] \equiv \text{argmax } U[x, I^0 - Px, 1 - N - t(k)]. \quad (2.43)$$

Because leisure at each given location is exogenous when work hours are fixed, the relation between housing and leisure can be defined as one of complements or substitutes, as $\partial x/\partial z \gtreqless 0$.[10] Other than its dependence upon $z$, (2.43) exhibits the usual Marshallian demand properties.

Location equilibrium is found in this model by substituting (2.43) into (2.42) and maximizing with respect to distance. The FOC reduces to a modified form of Muth's and Alonso's location choice equation,

$$-P_k x - c_k - [U_z/U_y]t_k = 0. \quad (2.44)$$

The MBD is the housing expenditure reduction from moving farther out, $-P_k x$. The MCD comprises the money cost of additional travel, $c_k$, and the value of time spent in additional travel, $[U_z/U_y]t_k$. The latter term measures the monetized value of leisure forgone by additional travel, since all additional travel time necessarily reduces leisure when work time is fixed at the level $N$.

Most of the analysis from here on can proceed as before. Since $U_z > 0$, (2.44) requires $P_k < 0$. The convexity result and comparative static predictions, though, require additional specification or restrictions on the utility function to make effects on $\text{MRS}_{z,y}$ determinate; this analysis is provided in full by Brown (1985).

---

## 2.3 LOCAL EMPLOYMENT

The analysis thus far assumes that all employment takes place in the CBD. Muth (1969: 42–45) also introduced local or non-CBD employment into the model. DeSalvo (1977a) provided a detailed study of the model and its implications.[11] My approach once again differs somewhat from these in that it emphasizes the fundamental duality between nonspatial and location demand theories.

## The Model

This model retains the monocentric CBD orientation, but in addition assumes that dispersed job sites exist throughout the urban area, particularly in the local service industry. To begin, ignore the leisure choice problem. The locally employed household residing and working at $k$ obtains income $I(k)$, where the characteristics of $I(k)$ are implications of equilibrium. The household faces housing price $P(k)$, where $P_k < 0$ holds by virtue of households employed in the CBD. The *locally employed* household's problem is therefore

$$\max_{x,y,k} U(x, y) \text{ s.t. } I(k) = P(k)x + y. \tag{2.45}$$

Notice that the locally employed household does not commute to work and therefore does not incur transportation costs.

Consumption equilibrium is defined by the Marshallian housing demand

$$x[P(k), I(k)] \equiv \operatorname{argmax} U[x, I(k) - P(k)x]. \tag{2.46}$$

The Marshallian housing demand exhibits the usual characteristics, with $\partial x/\partial P < 0$ and $\partial x/\partial I > 0$ under normality.

## Local Wage Income Gradient

Location equilibrium is found by substituting (2.46) into the objective function and maximizing with respect to $k$. The optimal location $k^*$ satisfies

$$V_P P_k + V_I I_k = 0. \tag{2.47}$$

The properties of the indirect utility function can be shown to hold: $V_P = -U_y x$ and $V_I = U_y$ so that (2.47) implies

$$-P_k x + I_k = 0. \tag{2.48}$$

This condition replaces Muth's equation in the CBD employment model. From it notice that $I_k$ must take the same sign as $P_k$: *Local wage income increases or decreases with distance as housing price increases or decreases with distance.* It is typically assumed that the urban area comprises both CBD-employed and locally employed households, with the presence of CBD-employed households ensuring $P_k < 0$. Therefore, $I_k < 0$, leading to the main prediction of the local employment model as usually stated in the literature: *Local wage income decreases with distance from the CBD.* The $-P_k x$ term is the MBD, whereas $I_k$ is now the MCD. The existence of local employment location equilibrium requires that wage income decline with distance to penalize the household for being able to avoid the CBD-oriented commuting costs while enjoying the lower housing price farther out. Although the paucity of wage-location data for private-sector employers has hampered empirical study of the intraurban wage gradient, Eberts (1981) presented some solid evidence of a metropolitan wage gradient for employees of various local governments scattered throughout the Chicago urban area. More recent evidence of negative wage gradients for private-sector workers has been found by Ihlanfeldt (1992).

The SOC for the maximization requires

$$-P_{kk}x - P_k(\partial x/\partial k) + I_{kk} < 0,$$

so that $P_{kk} > 0$ and $\partial x/\partial k > 0$ (see [2.49]) imply no restrictions on the wage income function convexity. Thus, $I(k)$ properties cannot be completely specified from the partial equilibrium model with local employment, a conclusion that may be surprising given the success in characterizing $P(k)$ completely in the earlier models.

Nonetheless, there is a result consistent with the CBD-employment models, that of increasing housing demand with distance. Differentiating (2.46) yields

$$\partial x/\partial k = (\partial x/\partial P)P_k + (\partial x/\partial I)I_k$$

$$= (\partial X/\partial P)P_k + (\partial x/\partial I)[-P_k x + I_k] \qquad (2.49)$$

$$= (\partial X/\partial P)P_k > 0,$$

where the second line follows by substituting the Slutsky equation and the third by (2.48) and the Substitution Theorem $\partial X/\partial P < 0$. Thus, *the housing demand of the locally employed household increases with distance*, as asserted.

### Comparative Statics

The comparative statics for the locally employed household, summarized in table 2.2, are identical to those of the CBD-employed household for housing price and tastes. Of course, there are no transportation costs here, but the changes in the CBD-employed household's net income $I^0(k) = I - T(k, I)$ induced by changes in $I$ or the form of $T(k, I)$ translate immediately into changes in the non-CBD-employed household's income $I(k)$. The behavioral parallels for the two models are reassuring because they demonstrate that location demand prop-

Table 2.2  COMPARATIVE STATICS FOR LOCALLY EMPLOYED HOUSEHOLD

| Increase in: | Sufficient Conditions | Muth's Model | | Leisure Model | |
|---|---|---|---|---|---|
| | | $x^*$ | $k^*$ | $x^*$ | $k^*$ |
| Housing price | $P_{k\alpha} \geq 0$ | — | — | ? | ? |
| | Marshallian complements | | | ? | ? |
| | Unrelated | | | — | — |
| | Substitutes | | | — | — |
| | $P_{k\alpha} < 0$ | ? | ? | ? | ? |
| Nonwage income | | + | + | | |
| | Hicksian complements | | | + | + |
| | Unrelated | | | + | + |
| | Substitutes | | | ? | ? |
| Wage | | ? | ? | ? | ? |
| | Consensus parameters | + | + or 0 | | |
| Housing tastes | | + | + | ? | ? |

erties are not fundamentally altered by the introduction of non-CBD work sites in the CBD-oriented housing market, and therefore suggest that these complications may be ignored in many applications.

## 2.4 LOCAL EMPLOYMENT AND LEISURE CHOICE

I now extend the analysis of section 2.3 to include labor-leisure choice, and demonstrate a fundamental difference between CBD employment and local employment when household time allocation is explicitly introduced. The CBD-employed household allocates time to three uses: work, leisure, and travel. The decision to spend more time traveling leaves less time available for work and leisure. The non-CBD-employed household, on the other hand, does not face the same time allocation problem; the decision to live *and work* farther from the CBD does not incur additional time cost of travel, leaving the total amount of time for labor and leisure unchanged. Thus, different labor supply gradients may be observed over distance for locally employed *versus* CBD-employed households.

### The Model

This model is a hybrid of the local employment and CBD-employed leisure choice models analyzed in Turnbull (1992b), and is closely related to the Sullivan (1983) and Straszheim (1984) models of job site choice. Following the CBD employment leisure choice model notation, household nonwage income remains $w_0$; the hourly wage, however, now depends upon location, $w(k)$. The wage gradient remains unspecified at this point.

Because the locally employed household spends no time commuting, total time is allocated between labor and leisure, $n + z = 1$, so that

$$n = 1 - z. \tag{2.50}$$

Total household income at $k$ is $w_0 + w(k)(1 - z)$, and the budget constraint becomes

$$I^0(k) = P(k)x + y + wz, \tag{2.51}$$

where $I^0(k) = w_0 + w(k)$ is total potential income to be "spent" on housing, nonhousing consumption, and leisure.

**Consumption Equilibrium**

The Marshallian demands are found in the usual way. The different structure of the model, however, justifies some intermediate derivation. The consumption problem is

$$\max_{x,y,z} U(x, y, z) \text{ s.t. } I^0(k) = P(k)x + y + wz.$$

The FOC are, with multiplier $\lambda$,

$$U_x - \lambda P = 0, \tag{2.52}$$

$$U_y - \lambda = 0, \tag{2.53}$$

$$U_z - \lambda w = 0, \text{ and} \tag{2.54}$$

$$I^0 - Px - y - wz = 0. \tag{2.55}$$

The Marshallian demands are the solutions to these conditions,

$$x[P(k), w(k), I^0(k)]; \ y[P(k), w(k), I^0(k)]; \ z[P(k), w(k), I^0(k)]. \tag{2.56}$$

These demand functions exhibit the usual characteristics with respect to $P$ and $I^0$. By construction, though, $\partial x/\partial w$ captures only the effect of wage changes as changes in the price of leisure, that is, holding $I^0$ unchanged. This approach allows the two effects of wage changes to be more easily separated—those of changes in the price of the good "leisure" from those of changes in potential money income (in contrast to changes in the purchasing power of given potential money income) $dI^0/dw$. This convention, of course, in no way affects the implications of the theory. It does, however, emphasize relationships that otherwise remain obscure.

Substitute (2.56) into the objective function to obtain the indirect utility function

$$V(P, w, I^0) = U[x(P, w, I^0), y(P, w, I^0), z(P, w, I^0)]. \quad (2.57)$$

Verifying its properties, differentiate with respect to $w$ (holding $I^0$ unchanged) to find

$$V_w = U_x(\partial x/\partial w) + U_y(\partial y/\partial w) + U_z(\partial z/\partial w). \quad (2.58)$$

Now substitute $U_x = \lambda P$, and so on, from (2.52) to (2.54):

$$V_w = \lambda[P(\partial x/\partial w) + (\partial y/\partial w) + w(\partial z/\partial w)]. \quad (2.59)$$

Substituting (2.56) into (2.55) and differentiating with respect to wage yields

$$-z = [P(\partial x/\partial w) + (\partial y/\partial w) + w(\partial z/\partial w)], \quad (2.60)$$

so that (2.59) becomes

$$V_w = -\lambda z. \quad (2.61)$$

Similar manipulations yield $V_p = -\lambda x$ and $V_{I^0} = \lambda$.

## Location Choice

The FOC for maximizing (2.57) with respect to location is

$$V_P P_k + V_w w_k + V_{I^0} w_k = 0.$$

Using the properties of $V$, this requires

$$\lambda[-P_k x - w_k z + w_k] = 0$$

or, using $\lambda > 0$ and $n = 1 - z$, one obtains

$$-P_k x + w_k n = 0. \quad (2.62)$$

This condition implies that the consumer locates where the change in housing cost ($P_k x$) equals the change in wage income ($w_k n$) from changing location. In general, *the local employment wage rate rises or falls as housing price rises or falls with distance.* If the city is monocentric with some CBD employment, though, $P_k < 0$ so that the location equilibrium condition (2.62) implies $w_k < 0$: *the wage rate declines with distance, as in the local employment model without leisure choice.* Here though, it cannot be concluded that *wage income* declines with distance without examining the labor supply gradient. In (2.62) the MCD is the decline in wage income from a given expenditure of time on labor as wage falls at greater distances from the CBD. The SOC requires that MBD intersect MCD from above, which again places no restriction on the convexity of $w(k)$. This much is consistent with the local employment model without leisure choice.

The housing demand gradient is found using (2.56):

$$\partial x/\partial k = (\partial x/\partial P)P_k + (\partial x/\partial w)w_k + (\partial x/\partial I^0)w_k.$$

Slutsky's equations for own-price and cross-price effects on housing are, respectively

$$\partial x/\partial P = \partial X/\partial P - x(\partial x/\partial I^0)$$
$$\partial x/\partial w = \partial X/\partial w - z(\partial x/\partial I^0),$$

so that substitution yields

$$\partial x/\partial k = (\partial X/\partial P)P_k + (\partial X/\partial w)w_k + (\partial x/\partial I^0)[-P_k x + w_k n].$$

Applying (2.62) reveals

$$\partial x/\partial k = (\partial X/\partial P)P_k + (\partial X/\partial w)w_k. \tag{2.63}$$

What is different here is that even though it is known that $\partial X/\partial P < 0$, $P_k < 0$, and that $w_k < 0$, the Hicksian housing demand response to the wage, $\partial X/\partial w$, can take either sign, depending upon the compensated relationship between housing and leisure. This ambiguity leaves the housing gradient ambiguous a priori, a result contrasting with housing gradient implications for all of the models considered previously.

In all the other models, spatial variation in housing demand arises from changes in relative housing price and net income alone; the net effect reflects on the compensated change in housing price across distance in the neighborhood of the optimal location. In this model, on the other hand, the net effect reflects compensated changes in both relative housing and leisure prices across distance. Increasing distance from the CBD lowers housing price, which increases housing demand. At the same time, though, one must recognize that increasing distance also lowers the wage rate, decreasing the price of leisure. If leisure and housing are complements, then the simultaneous decrease in housing and leisure relative prices reinforces each other's effects on housing demand, therefore unambiguously increasing housing demand with distance. On the other hand, if leisure and housing are substitutes, then the simultaneous decrease in housing and leisure relative prices offsets each other's effects: the decreasing price of leisure reduces housing demand, offsetting the effect of decreasing housing price on housing demand and leaving (2.63) ambiguous.

Differentiate the Marshallian demand for leisure (2.56) to find the leisure-distance relationship

$$\partial z/\partial k = (\partial z/\partial P)P_k + (\partial z/\partial w)w_k + (\partial z/\partial I^o)w_k.$$

The relevant Slutsky equations for Marshallian leisure demand in this model can be shown to be

$$\partial z/\partial P = \partial Z/\partial P - x(\partial z/\partial I^o)$$
$$\partial z/\partial w = \partial Z/\partial w - z(\partial z/\partial I^o),$$

so that the leisure-distance relationship becomes, with substitution,

$$\partial z/\partial k = (\partial Z/\partial P)P_k + (\partial Z/\partial w)w_k + (\partial z/\partial I^o)[-P_k x + w_k n].$$

The last term is zero by (2.62), resulting in

$$\partial z/\partial k = (\partial Z/\partial P)P_k + (\partial Z/\partial w)w_k. \tag{2.64}$$

The spatial variation in leisure demand comprises two possibly offsetting effects. The first term captures how spatial variation in housing price affects leisure demand, while the second term captures how spatial variation in the wage rate affects leisure demand. The Hicksian demand property is $\partial Z/\partial w < 0$, so that the latter effect of wage on leisure is clearcut: decreasing wage with distance prompts greater leisure demand with distance. Therefore, if leisure and housing are complements in the nonspatial Hicksian demand sense, then $\partial Z/\partial P < 0$ and spatial variation in the housing price reinforces the effect of spatial variation in wage on leisure. If they are substitutes, however, the decrease in housing price with distance reduces leisure demand, offsetting the positive effect of declining wage. The conditions underlying the signs of housing and leisure gradient slopes are, not surprisingly, identical.

Finally, since $n = 1 - z$, the labor supply gradient follows

$$\partial n/\partial k = -\partial z/\partial k. \tag{2.65}$$

Herein lies another result contrasting with the centrally employed household case. *Whereas the labor supply gradient for the CBD-employed household depends upon the spatial variation in both leisure demand and travel time, the labor supply gradient for the locally employed household depends solely upon the spatial variation in leisure demand.* The result holds because, intuitively, the locally employed household spends no time commuting to work.

But what can be concluded about the propensity of locally employed households to consume leisure relative to their CBD-employed
counterparts? Consider two identical households, A (CBD-employed)
and B (locally employed), both residing at the same distance from the
CBD, $k^*$, in equilibrium. Concentrating upon leisure consumption,
define the composite commodity $Q = P(k^*)x + y$; because both
households face the same housing price at $k^*$, the price normalization
condition for Q holds for both households under consideration. Nonetheless, the implication of this construct is that each household's consumption choice problem can be seen as the choice between z and Q,
as depicted in figure 2.4.

Since both households are identical (other than their employment
sites), they both attain utility $U^*$ when selecting their respective optimal consumption bundles of leisure and Q. The slope of the budget
line facing A in the figure is the negative of the relative price of leisure,
the CBD wage $w(0)$. This household is in equilibrium at $k^*$ consuming
$(z^A, Q^A)$.

Figure 2.4  COMPARING LEISURE DEMAND FOR CENTRAL BUSINESS DISTRICT
           AND LOCALLY EMPLOYED HOUSEHOLDS

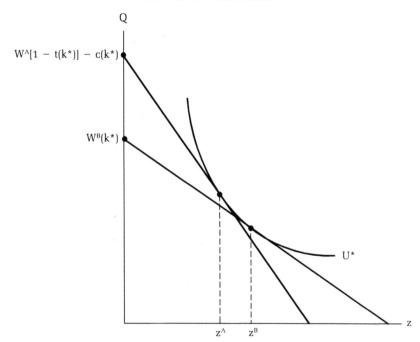

The slope of the budget line facing household $B$ in the figure is the negative of the relative price of leisure at $k^*$, the local employment wage $w(k^*)$. This household is in equilibrium at $k^*$ consuming $(z^B, Q^B)$. Since $w_k < 0$, $w(k^*) < w(0)$ and the budget line for $B$ is shallower than that for A. It immediately follows that household $B$ chooses to consume more leisure than $A$; graphing leisure demand against distance, the locally employed consumer leisure gradient lies above that of the CBD-employed consumer at each location.

## Comparative Statics

It turns out that the comparative static predictions for the local employment model with leisure choice also differ from the results established earlier for CBD employment models. To illustrate, introduce the shift parameter $\alpha$ into the model and evaluate the comparative static responses to $d\alpha > 0$. The results are summarized in table 2.2.

### HOUSING PRICE CHANGES

Putting $\alpha$ into the housing price function, with $P_\alpha > 0$, the effects on Marshallian demands are $\partial x/\partial\alpha = (\partial x/\partial P)P_\alpha$ and $\partial z/\partial\alpha = (\partial z/\partial P)P_\alpha$. Thus, the housing demand gradient shifts downward, whereas the leisure demand gradient shifts upward or downward according to whether leisure and housing are Marshallian substitutes or complements.

The effect on household location is found from (2.62) to be

$$dk^*/d\alpha = [P_{k\alpha}x + P_kP_\alpha(\partial x/\partial P) + w_kP_\alpha(\partial z/\partial P)]\lambda/V_{kk}. \quad (2.66)$$

The first two terms should look familiar; they capture the net effect of price function rotation and shift on MBD. The third term, however, is new; it captures the effect of $\alpha$ on MCD. To trace out the effect on MCD, note that leisure is endogenous, so that any change in $P(k)$ changes leisure demand, that is, labor supply, as well. But the change in labor supply changes the marginal wage income cost of moving farther away from the CBD. If leisure is a complement (substitute) with housing, MCD rises (falls), which by itself prompts the household to locate closer in (farther out). Whether this change in MCD reinforces or offsets the MBD effect on location demand depends upon the sign of the first two terms in (2.66), that is, the relative strength of the price function rotation.

## TASTE CHANGES

In the other models, taste changes had their effects on location only through changes in MBD. Here, on the other hand, a possible effect of taste on MCD (via leisure demand, hence labor supply) again complicates the comparative statics.

Introduce $\alpha$ as the taste parameter into the Marshallian housing and leisure demands, then differentiate the location choice FOC to obtain

$$dk^*/d\alpha = [P_k(\partial x/\partial \alpha) + w_k(\partial z/\partial \alpha)]\lambda/V_{kk}. \qquad (2.67)$$

As before, stronger taste for housing $(\partial x/\partial \alpha > 0)$ increases the MBD, prodding the household to locate farther out. However, the effect of taste upon leisure demand must also be considered. If the taste for leisure becomes stronger as well, $\partial z/\partial \alpha > 0$ and the MCD falls and the household locates closer to the CBD. If the taste for leisure weakens, $\partial z/\partial \alpha < 0$ and the MCD rises and the household resides farther out. *Thus, only when $\partial z/\partial \alpha \leq 0$ can one unambiguously conclude that the optimal location is farther away from the CBD.* This is quite unlike the CBD-employed household case, in which stronger taste for housing prompts a move farther out regardless of the effect on leisure demand (see previous subsection on "Comparative Statics with Endogenous Labor Supply," in section 2.2.).

## INCOME CHANGES

The last set of comparative statics is that relating to changes in non-wage and wage income. Consider the former. Under normality, $\partial z/\partial w_0 > 0$. Thus, differentiating the location choice FOC (2.62) yields

$$dk^*/dw_0 = [P_k(\partial x/\partial w_0) + w_k(\partial z/\partial w_0)]\lambda/V_{kk} > 0. \qquad (2.68)$$

Greater nonwage income stimulates housing demand, which in turn increases MBD and the household moves farther out. At the same time, greater nonwage income stimulates leisure demand, which in turn decreases MCD and the household moves farther out, reinforcing the MBD effect on location.

Substituting $k^*$ into the Marshallian housing and leisure demands and differentiating yields:

$$dx^*/dw_0 = \partial x/\partial w_0 + (\partial x/\partial k)(dk^*/dw_0) \qquad (2.69)$$

$$dz^*/dw_0 = \partial z/\partial w_0 + (\partial z/\partial k)(dk^*/dw_0). \qquad (2.70)$$

The first right-hand side terms in (2.69) and (2.70) are the direct (and positive) effects of $w_0$ on housing and leisure demands. The second terms are the location effects. Since $\partial x/\partial k$ and $\partial z/\partial k$ are ambiguous a priori, the total effect of $w_0$ on x and z remains ambiguous as well. For the case *where housing and leisure are Hicksian complements or unrelated, though, $\partial x/\partial k > 0$ and $\partial z/\partial k > 0$, so that location effects reinforce direct effects and households with higher nonwage income consume more housing and leisure farther out.* When housing and leisure are Hicksian substitutes, however, it may be possible that $\partial x/\partial k < 0$ and/or $\partial z/\partial k < 0$, leaving offsetting location effects of nonwage income in (2.69) and (2.70).

Given that the local employment wage rate varies by location, changes in the wage function entail shifts with rotation in general. Introducing the shift parameter $\alpha$, specify $w(k, \alpha)$ where $w_\alpha > 0$ indicates an increase in local wages at all locations while the sign of $w_{k\alpha}$ indicates the direction of wage function rotation.

Because $I^0 = w_0 + w(k, \alpha)$, the effects of local wage function changes on Marshallian housing demand and leisure demand are

$$\partial x/\partial \alpha = (\partial x/\partial w)w_\alpha + (\partial x/\partial I^0)w_\alpha \tag{2.71}$$

$$\partial z/\partial \alpha = (\partial z/\partial w)w_\alpha + (\partial z/\partial I^0)w_\alpha. \tag{2.72}$$

The Slutsky equations yield $\partial x/\partial w = \partial X/\partial w - z(\partial x\partial I^0)$ and $\partial z/\partial w = \partial Z/\partial w - z(\partial z/\partial I^0)$ so that, with substitution (2.71) and (2.72) become, respectively:

$$\partial x/\partial \alpha = (\partial X/\partial w)w_\alpha + n(\partial x/\partial I^0)w_\alpha \tag{2.73}$$

$$\partial z/\partial \alpha = (\partial Z/\partial w)w_\alpha + n(\partial z/\partial I^0)w_\alpha. \tag{2.74}$$

An increase in wage has ambiguous effects on both housing and leisure Marshallian demands, which translate into ambiguous changes in MBD and MCD. Further restrictions on the model, with respect to housing-leisure relationships in demand as well as the responsiveness of labor supply to wage changes, must be imposed to generate determinate location and housing and leisure choice comparative statics for changes in the wage function.

## Work Time Constraints

Recall that the introduction of fixed work time, N, reduces Muth's modified CBD-employment with leisure choice model to Alonso's variant. Does the introduction of N have similar consequences here? Interestingly, the answer is no.

To see why, notice that with local employment and no commuting time, leisure is simply $z = 1 - n$. Setting $n = N$ therefore leaves one with fixed leisure time, $z = 1 - N$, and the household's problem becomes

$$\max_{x,y,k} U(x, y, 1 - N) \text{ s.t. } w_0 + w(k)N = P(k)x + y. \quad (2.75)$$

Since $1 - N$ is fixed, problem (2.75) is identical with the local employment model without leisure choice studied in section 2.3. Thus, the conclusions of that model hold here as well.

---

## 2.5 CONCLUDING REMARKS

This chapter has presented a comprehensive review of urban household location demand theory, beginning with the simplest formulation in which all urban area employment is located in the CBD, then extending the model to include the complications introduced by leisure-labor choice as well as local or non-CBD employment opportunities. Various developments and modifications to urban consumer theory appearing in the literature have been discussed within the unifying theme of location theory and neoclassical nonspatial demand theory duality.

A wide degree of conformity can be observed among the implications of the different models. For example, looking at tables 2.1 and 2.2, the simple model of the CBD-employed household, the CBD-employed household with labor-leisure choice, and the locally employed household (without leisure choice) all generate similar housing price, transportation cost, and income comparative statics. Many of the comparative statics are ambiguous in the model of the locally employed household with leisure choice, in contrast to the stronger predictions of the other models. Still, none of these comparative statics contradicts the others.

The consumer models presented in this chapter have been formally posited to pertain to household behavior in the monocentric urban area. It turns out, though, that the picture of household behavior need not change for multiple CBD cities, or cities with beltline employment centers (e.g., White 1976, Weiland 1987, Yinger 1992b, and Turnbull 1993b). What does change is the interpretation of the results. For example, distance $k$ can represent the length of a household's commute to the job site—whether to the CBD or some other employment site in the urban area. The theory nonetheless implies that households commute "up" the housing price function to their job site, a partial equilibrium result that, in turn, allows the delineation of spatial groupings of types of households (by work site) when aggregating to the market level of analysis.

The partial equilibrium models presented here can also be extended to incorporate the effects of transportation system congestion or location-specific amenities. The effects of congestion per se can be introduced as an exogenous (to the household) shift in the shape of the transportation cost function. Likewise, the introduction of high-speed limited-access commuting routes can be introduced by altering the location index interpretation to "effective distance" rather than measured distance. It is at the market level of aggregation that these extensions create modeling difficulties, not at the partial equilibrium level (e.g., Solow and Vickery 1971).

Location-specific amenities can be similarly introduced into the model (Yamada 1972). To illustrate, if the amenity at location $k$ is denoted $A(k)$, then the utility function can be modified to take into account consumer preference for $A(k)$, using $U(x, y, A(k))$.[12] Replacing the standard "Muth" utility function employed in the chapter, $U(x, y)$, with this utility function, results can be derived following the Alonso version of the consumer model explained in the subsection "Work Time Constraints," in section 2.2.

Finally, the theoretical motivation for this chapter deserves reemphasizing. Just as partial equilibrium neoclassical consumer theory provides the foundation for nonspatial market-level analysis, the partial equilibrium location theory studied in this chapter provides the foundation upon which market-level spatial models are built. A firm grounding in partial equilibrium certainty theory is therefore necessary before studying the interesting questions occupying prominent positions in the literature. With this end in mind, this chapter's survey provided greater emphasis upon modeling than is typically found in other literature surveys.

---

### APPENDIX 2A:  PROPERTIES OF THE INDIRECT UTILITY FUNCTION

This appendix demonstrates the properties of the indirect utility function, $V(P, I^0)$, used in chapter 2. For example, consider the consumption choice problem (2.2):

$$\max_{x,y} U(x, y) \text{ s.t. } I^0 = Px + y. \tag{A.1}$$

The Lagrangian function is

$$L(x, y, \lambda) = U(x, y) + [I^0 - Px - y]. \qquad (A.2)$$

The FOC are $\partial L/\partial x = \partial L/\partial y = \partial L/\partial \lambda = 0$, which can be rearranged to the following, respectively:

$$U_x = \lambda P, \qquad (A.3)$$

$$U_y = \lambda, \text{ and} \qquad (A.4)$$

$$I^0 = Px + y. \qquad (A.5)$$

The solutions to these conditions are $x(P, I^0)$, $y(P, I^0)$, and $\lambda(P, I^0)$. Substitute these values into (A.5), then differentiate with respect to $P$ to obtain

$$-x(P, I^0) = P(\partial x/\partial P) + (\partial y/\partial P). \qquad (A.6)$$

Similarly, differentiate (A.5) with respect to $I^0$ to obtain

$$1 = P(\partial x/\partial I^0) + (\partial y/\partial I^0). \qquad (A.7)$$

Now define the indirect utility function (2.3)

$$V(P, I^0) \equiv U[x(P, I^0), y(P, I^0)]. \qquad (A.8)$$

Differentiate indirect utility with respect to $P$ to find

$$\begin{aligned} V_P &= U_x(\partial x/\partial P) + U_y(\partial y/\partial P) \\ &= \lambda[P(\partial x/\partial P) + (\partial y/\partial P)] = -\lambda x(P, I^0), \end{aligned} \qquad (A.9)$$

where (A.3) and (A.4) are substituted into (A.9) to obtain the second equality and (A.7) is used to obtain the third equality. Thus $V_P = -\lambda x$, as asserted in the text.

One can similarly show $V_I = \lambda$. Differentiate indirect utility (A.8) with respect to $I^0$ to find

$$V_I = U_x(\partial x/\partial I^0) + U_y(\partial y/\partial I^0) = \lambda[P(\partial x/\partial I^0) + (\partial y/\partial I^0)] = \lambda, \quad (A.10)$$

where (A.3) and (A.4) are substituted into (A.10) to obtain the second equality, and (A.7) is used to obtain the third equality. Thus, $V_I = \lambda$.

Finally, several places in the chapter use the fact that $\lambda > 0$, which follows from the FOC $U_y = \lambda$ and the assumption that the marginal utility of $y$ is positive.

---

**Notes**

1. See, for example, Alonso (1964), Mills (1967; 1972), Muth (1969), Wheaton (1974), Hartwick et al. (1976), and Brueckner (1987) for models of the monocentric urban

residential land market and, for example, White (1976), Weiland (1987), Yinger (1992b), and Turnbull (1993b, c) for models of the urban land market with multiple employment centers.

2. Note that Muth's equation (2.6) is $V_k/\lambda = 0$ at the maximizing location $k^*$. The SOC for a maximum $V$ is $V_{kk} < 0$, so that the derivative of $V_k/\lambda$ with respect to $k$ is $D = -(\partial\lambda/\partial k)V_k/\lambda^2 + V_{kk}/\lambda = V_{kk}/\lambda$, where the second equality follows because $V_k = 0$ at $k^*$.

3. The general comparative statics for this version of the model have been worked out in detail by Muth (1969) and DeSalvo (1977b). The comparative statics for the other variants considered throughout this chapter have been worked out by Brown (1985), DeSalvo (1977a, 1985), and Turnbull (1992b).

4. Table 2.1 summarizes the comparative statics derived below for ease of reference.

5. Recall that Muth's equation is $V_k/\lambda = 0$, so that the derivative with respect to $k$ yields $V_{kk}/\lambda$ using $V_k = 0$ at $k^*$.

6. See Blackley and Follain (1983: 509–10) for an example of this case. Interpreting $P(k)$ as the user cost of housing in the steady state, they show how an increase in the expected inflation rate increases the nominal interest rate and therefore shifts $P(k)$ upward and steepens the slope when the impact of mortgage interest deductibility for income taxes is included in the model.

7. Muth (1969) and DeSalvo (1977b) modeled taste changes as changes in $\mathrm{MRS}_{x,y}$. My approach is consistent with theirs, since the household consumes more housing at a given location, prices, and income as tastes for housing become stronger in Muth's model.

8. Define the Lagrangian for (2.28) as $L(x, y, z, \lambda) = U(x, y, z) + \lambda[I^0 - Px - y - wz]$. The FOC are $\partial L/\partial x = \partial L/\partial y = \partial L/\partial z = \partial L/\partial\lambda = 0$, which yield, respectively: $U_x = \lambda P$; $U_y = \lambda$; $U_z = \lambda w$; and $I^0 = Px + y + wz$. Rearranging yields the conditions stated in the text: $U_x/U_y = P$ and $U_z/U_y = w$.

9. Compare this to DeSalvo's (1985) result. DeSalvo specifies taste changes as altering $\mathrm{MRS}_{x,y}$, but must constrain the impact on the trade-off between housing and leisure and leisure and nonhousing to obtain determinate results.

10. The FOC to (2.43) requires that $\mathrm{MRS}_{x,y} = P$. Differentiating this condition reveals that the sign of $\partial x/\partial z$ follows that of $d\mathrm{MRS}_{x,y}/dz$; increasing (decreasing) $\mathrm{MRS}_{x,y}$ with leisure leads to greater (less) housing demand.

11. See White (1976, 1978) for other analyses with non-CBD employment sites.

12. The location-specific amenity model has been used to study racial segregation when consumers have preferences over the racial composition of their neighborhoods. See, for example, Yinger (1976, 1992a), Courant and Yinger (1977), and Kern (1981).

# Chapter Three

# THE PUBLIC SECTOR AND
# HOUSEHOLD BEHAVIOR

This chapter introduces a taxing, regulating, and service-providing local public sector into the model to see how these factors modify the implications of the theory. The focus of analysis remains consumer housing and location demand behavior, and responses to specific public sector influences. Retaining the partial equilibrium perspective has several advantages at this stage. As before, of course, understanding spatial housing market equilibrium outcomes requires a well-developed theory of agent behavior. But even more important for this application, the partial equilibrium approach permits dispensing with the more stringent assumptions on functional forms, and so on, that are needed to generate equilibrium city-level results;[1] urban households are not assumed identical, as is typically the case in more aggregated analysis, and no specific functional forms are assumed. Still, the partial equilibrium analysis is seriously incomplete because it neglects the consumer's choice of the jurisdiction within which to reside, public facilities congestion, externalities, and other spatial effects. Nonetheless, the partial equilibrium model of consumer behavior represents a good starting point for more complete rigorous analyses.

The two broad areas of public-sector influence studied in this chapter cover taxing and service-providing activities, and housing subsidy policies. Sections 3.1 and 3.2 address the taxing and spending functions of government, considering exogenous and endogenous government fiscal policy, respectively. Section 3.3 examines the effect of direct housing policies that establish minimum consumption standards and subsidies, and section 3.4 presents conclusions.

## 3.1 LOCAL TAXES AND PUBLIC SERVICES

Consider the case where the entire urban area falls within a single local jurisdiction so that public service levels and tax rates do not vary by location. The public-sector variables are exogenous to the consumer; the endogenous public-sector model is considered in the next section.

All notation remains as defined in chapter 2, but with the additional terms: $\rho$ = property tax rate; $\delta$ = sales tax rate; $\tau$ = income tax rate; $g$ = public service; $r$ = consumer price of housing (which may differ from the market price $P$ by the tax wedge); and $q$ = consumer price of other goods. Utility is now $U(x, y, g)$, with more $g$ being preferred to less, or $\partial U/\partial g = U_g > 0$. As before, the producer price of $y$ is normalized to unity so that

$$q = 1 + \delta. \tag{3.1}$$

The consumer price of housing takes a bit more development. Suppose the asset price (per unit of housing) of property, capital and land, used for residential purposes is $R$. Then, if the interest rate is $i$ and the income tax rate is $\tau$, the consumer rental price of housing is

$$r = [i(1 - \tau) + \rho(1 - \tau)]R, \tag{3.2}$$

assuming the interest cost and property tax are fully deductible for income tax purposes.[2] The term $i(1 - \tau)$ is the after-tax financing cost, and $\rho(1 - \tau)$ is the property tax cost per dollar of housing; $[i + \rho](1 - \tau)$ is the after tax user cost of a dollar's worth of housing capital stock.

The producer rental price of housing, the annualized cost of additions to the housing stock, satisfies $P = iR$ in equilibrium, or

$$R = P/i. \tag{3.3}$$

Substituting (3.3) into (3.2) reveals the relation between the consumer price of housing and the producer price of housing as

$$r = [1 + (\rho/i)](1 - \tau)P,$$

which simplifies to, recalling that housing rental price is a function of distance,

$$r(k) = P(k)[1 + \gamma](1 - \tau), \tag{3.4}$$

where $\gamma = \rho/i$ is now the capitalized property tax rate.

## Consumption Equilibrium

Given the income tax rate, $\tau$, net income is $I(1 - \tau)$, so that the consumer's budget constraint becomes, using (3.1) and (3.4):[3]

$$I(1 - \tau) = r(k)x + qy + T[k, I(1 - \tau)] \tag{3.5}$$
$$I(1 - \tau) = P(k)(1 + \gamma)(1 - \tau)x$$

The Marshallian demands are therefore

$[x(r, q, I^o, g), y(r, q, I^o, g)]$

$$\equiv \text{argmax } [U(x, y, g) \text{ s.t. } I^o = rx + qy], \tag{3.6}$$

where $I^o = I(1 - \tau) - T[k, I(1 - \tau)]$ and r and q are given by (3.4) and (3.1). The Hicksian or compensated demands are

$[X(r, q, U^o, g), Y(r, q, U^o, g)]$

$$\equiv \text{argmin } [rx + qy \text{ s.t. } U^o = U(x, y, g)]. \tag{3.7}$$

Except for the inclusion of the public service g as an argument in each, (3.6) and (3.7) are the familiar nonspatial "ordinary" and "compensated" demands, respectively. Using the change of notation for consumer prices, the usual properties pertain. Concentrating on housing demand, and knowing that the Substitution Theorem, symmetry, and Slutsky's equation hold:

$$\partial X/\partial r < 0, \tag{3.8}$$

$$\partial X/\partial q = \partial Y/\partial r < 0, \text{ and} \tag{3.9}$$

$$\partial x/\partial r = \partial X/\partial r - x(\partial x/\partial I^o). \tag{3.10}$$

What is new is the introduction of the Marshallian demand relationship between the public service and housing. For this study's purposes define:

$$x, g \text{ are} \begin{cases} \text{complements} \\ \text{unrelated} \\ \text{substitutes} \end{cases} \text{ as } \partial x/\partial g \gtreqqless 0. \tag{3.11}$$

By definition, public services are categorized here as complements or substitutes with housing, depending upon whether the public services by themselves serve to increase or decrease housing demand, holding location unchanged.

Using (3.1) and (3.2) in (3.8)–(3.10), tax rate effects are, respectively:

$$\partial x/\partial \delta = \partial x/\partial q \gtreqqless 0 \tag{3.12}$$

$$\partial x/\partial \gamma = (\partial x/\partial r)(1 - \tau) < 0 \tag{3.13}$$

$$\partial x/\partial \tau = -(\partial x/\partial r)(1 + \gamma) - (\partial x/\partial I^o)I[1 - T_I] \gtreqqless 0, \tag{3.14}$$

where normality, $\partial x/\partial I^0 > 0$, is assumed throughout. Result (3.12) is straightforward; since an increase in the sales tax rate $\delta$ increases the consumer price of nonhousing goods, Marshallian housing demand responds as it would to changes in the price of y. Result (3.13) is similarly clear. Result (3.14), on the other hand, requires additional consideration.

Looking at the second additive term in (3.14), notice $[1 - T_I] > 0$, assuming that increases in wage income increase the total time cost of travel by less than the implied increase in potential wage income—that is, net of transportation cost money income increases at all locations when wage income rises, a reasonable characterization. Under normality, $\partial x/\partial I^0 > 0$ as well, so that the entire second term in (3.14) is negative. In sum, an increase in the income tax rate lowers money income net of transportation cost and taxes, thus lowering housing demand at the given location.

At the same time, however, the increase in $\tau$ increases the tax savings generated by the interest expenditures and the property tax bill associated with each unit of housing consumed. Thus an increase in $\tau$ reduces the net-of-tax consumer rental price of housing, which in turn increases the demand for housing at the given location. The first additive term in (3.14) captures this effect: $\partial x/\partial r < 0$, so that the entire first term is positive, as anticipated.

The income tax rate effect on Marshallian housing demand comprises these two offsetting influences and therefore remains ambiguous a priori. Not surprisingly, this ambiguity leads to ambiguous income tax effects on location and spatial housing demand, as illustrated in the subsections following.

## Location Choice

Following established procedure, substitute (3.6) into the utility function to obtain the indirect utility function $V(r, q, I^0)$, for which the usual properties pertain: $V_r = -\lambda x$, $V_q = -\lambda y$, and $V_I = \lambda$, where $\lambda$ is the Lagrangian multiplier from the utility maximization problem in (3.6), which follows by application of the envelope theorem. The optimal location $k^*$ satisfies

$$V_r r_k - V_I T_k = 0,$$

using $r_k = \partial r/\partial k$ from (3.4). This condition reduces to the usual form of Muth's equation

$$-r_k x - T_k = 0 \qquad (3.15)$$

or

$$-P_k(1 + \gamma)(1 - \tau)x - T_k = 0. \tag{3.16}$$

From these conditions the familiar decreasing convex housing price functions r(k) and P(k) can be demonstrated.

Similarly, the Marshallian housing demand is increasing in distance. Differentiating (3.6) reveals

$$\partial x/\partial k = (\partial x/\partial r)r_k - (\partial x/\partial I^0)T_k \tag{3.17}$$

$$= (\partial X/\partial r)r_k + (\partial x/\partial I^0)(-r_k x - T_k)$$

$$= (\partial X/\partial r)r_k > 0,$$

where the second line follows from (3.10) and the third from (3.15) and (3.8).

## Property Tax Effects

I now examine the comparative statics derived from the model, summarized in table 3.1. An increase in the property tax shifts the consumer housing price function (3.4) upward while making it steeper:

$$\partial r/\partial\gamma = P(k)(1 - \tau) > 0, \partial^2 r/\partial k\partial\gamma = P_k(k)(1 - \tau) < 0. \tag{3.18}$$

Table 3.1  TAX AND GOVERNMENT SERVICE COMPARATIVE STATICS

| Policy | Sufficient Conditions | Housing x* | Location k* |
|---|---|---|---|
| Property tax | Marshallian demand price elastic | ? | — |
| | Unit elastic | — | 0 |
| | Price inelastic | — | + |
| Sales tax | Marshallian substitutes | + | + |
| | Unrelated | 0 | 0 |
| | Complements | — | — |
| Income tax | | ? | ? |
| Interest deductibility | Marshallian demand price elastic | ? | + |
| | Unit elastic | 0 | 0 |
| | Price inelastic | — | — |
| Public service | Marshallian substitutes | — | — |
| | Unrelated | 0 | 0 |
| | Complements | + | + |

Note: Policy changes are listed as increases in tax rates, deductibility, and public services.

From the theory presented in chapter 2, it is known that such a change in housing price yields ambiguous comparative statics. The specific change in r implied by the way $\gamma$ enters the model, though, does permit further analysis.

Differentiate (3.15) or (3.16) with respect to $\gamma$ to obtain the capitalized property tax rate effect on location demand

$$dk^*/d\gamma = [P_k(1 - \tau)x + r_k P(k)(1 - \tau)(\partial x/\partial r)]/J, \qquad (3.19)$$

where $J = -r_{kk}x - r_k^2(\partial x/\partial r) - T_{kk} < 0$ from the SOC. To recast (3.19) in elasticity terms, rearrange the numerator using $r_k = P_k(1 + \gamma)(1 - \tau)$:

$$dk^*/d\gamma = [1 + (\partial x/\partial r)(r/x)]P_k(1 - \tau)x/J$$
$$= [1 + E(x, r)]P_k(1 - \tau)x/J, \qquad (3.20)$$

with $E(x, r)$ denoting the Marshallian price elasticity of demand from (3.20):

$$dk^*/d\gamma \gtreqless 0 \text{ as } |E(x, r)| \lesseqgtr 1. \qquad (3.21)$$

This result has intuitive appeal. If Marshallian housing demand is price inelastic, then the increase in housing price function slope (the first additive term in [3.19]) increases the housing expenditure savings more than the decrease in housing demand induced by the upward shift in r(k) (the second additive term in [3.19]), thus increasing marginal benefit of distance (MBD) and prompting the household to reside farther from the central business district (CBD). If housing demand is elastic, then the decrease in housing demand induced by the upward shift in r(k) outweighs the effect of the steeper r(k) slope and the MBD falls—with the result that the household finds CBD proximity more appealing.

So, what does this knowledge of parameter estimates suggest? The consensus is that housing demand is price inelastic (Mayo 1981), by (3.21) implying that $dk^*/d\gamma > 0$: *under a higher property tax rate, the household will live farther away from the CBD.*

Turning now to the effect of the property tax on spatial housing demand, substitute $k^*$ into (3.6) to find

$$x^* = x[r(k^*), q, I^0(k^*), g], \qquad (3.22)$$

so that taking the total derivative with respect to $\gamma$ reveals

$$dx^*/d\gamma = (\partial x/\partial r)P(k)(1 - \tau) + (\partial X/\partial r)r_k(dk^*/d\gamma), \qquad (3.23)$$

where (3.17) is used to derive the second term. The first term in (3.23) is the direct effect of the tax rate on housing demand, which is negative. The second term is the location effect. $|E(x, r)| \geq 1$ is sufficient to establish that the household reduces housing consumption when the property tax rate increases. In this case the increase in $\gamma$ prods the household to reside closer to the CBD, farther up the housing price function, the effect of which reinforces the tendency to reduce housing demand at each distance, due to the direct effect of the tax. On the other hand, if $|E(x, r)| < 1$, then the location effect offsets the direct effect of $\gamma$; as the household moves outward, down the housing price surface, the lower housing price farther out serves to offset the direct effect of $\gamma$ on housing demand at each location.

The property tax effect on housing consumption depends upon the relative strengths of the direct and location effects because housing demand is inelastic. Further, income and taste differences aside, it is even possible that households at one initial location increase housing consumption, while households at other locations do just the opposite. To see why, rearrange (3.23) into elasticity terms, multiplying both sides by $\gamma r/xr$ and the last right-hand-side term by $k/k$ as well to get

$$(dx^*/dk)(\gamma/x) = [(\partial x/\partial r)r/x][P(1 - \tau)\gamma/r]$$

$$+ [(\partial X/\partial r)r/x][r_k k/r][(dk^*/d\gamma)\gamma/k]. \quad (3.24)$$

Using $r_\gamma = P(k)(1 - \tau)$, (3.24) becomes in elasticity notation:

$$E(x^*, \gamma) = E(x, r)E(r, \gamma) + E(X, r)E(k^*, \gamma). \quad (3.25)$$

Since $E(r, \gamma) = \gamma/(1 + \gamma)$, this term is spatially constant. It is known that $E(x, r) < 0$ and $E(X, r) < 0$ and $E(k^*, \gamma) \gtrless 0$ as $|E(x, r)| \lesseqgtr 1$ from (3.21). Suppose $|E(x, r)| < 1$, as the empirical evidence suggests. If the demand and distance elasticities are spatially constant, the convexity of $r(k)$ ensures that $E(r, k)$ falls with distance, leading to a weaker second additive term (location effect) on the right-hand-side of (3.25) at the urban periphery than closer to the CBD. Because the location effect is positive in this example, offsetting the direct property tax effect on housing demand, this means that the location effect is at its weakest at the urban periphery and at its strongest at the CBD. Thus, it is entirely possible that $E(x^*, \gamma) > 0$ at the CBD whereas $E(x^*, \gamma) < 0$ farther out in the urban area; households proximate to the CBD increase housing consumption while their more outlying counterparts reduce consumption in response to the same property tax rate change.

## Sales Tax Effects

The sales tax effect is much more straightforward. From (3.15) the location response is

$$dk^*/d\delta = r_k(\partial x/\partial q)/J \gtreqless 0 \text{ as } \partial x/\partial q \gtreqless 0. \qquad (3.26)$$

If housing and nonhousing goods are Marshallian substitutes, then an increase in sales tax rate $\delta$ increases housing demand at each distance, increasing the MBD and optimal distance. The opposite occurs when they are complementary goods.[4]

Deriving housing demand change in the usual way, (3.22) yields

$$\begin{aligned} dx^*/d\delta &= (\partial x/\partial q) + (\partial X/\partial r)r_k(dk^*/d\delta) \\ &= (\partial x/\partial q)[1 + (\partial X/\partial r)r_k^2/J], \end{aligned} \qquad (3.27)$$

the sign of which follows the nonspatial cross-price effect, $\partial x/\partial q$. *The location effect always reinforces the direct effect of $\delta$ on housing demand, leading to the total effect reflective of the x − y demand relationship.*

### Income Tax Effects

Given that $\partial x/\partial\tau$ is in general ambiguous, it should not be surprising that all comparative statics for $k^*$ and $x^*$ are ambiguous as well, without additional model specification. What has received more interest in the literature is not the effect of the income tax per se, but the effect of the implicit subsidy to housing from income tax deductibility of interest and property taxes.

Muth (1969: 104) argued that, because the income tax deductibility of interest and property tax lowers the after-tax user cost of housing, it stimulates housing demand, thereby increasing the MBD so that households locate farther away from the CBD. According to this argument, the individual income tax indirectly feeds the postwar suburbanization process observed in the United States.

But this line of argument, undertaken without explicit location demand modeling, misses some important theoretical connections. Following Blackley and Follain (1983), introduce a deductibility parameter $\beta$, such that $\beta = 1$ when interest and property taxes are fully deductible and $\beta < 1$ when they are only partially deductible for income tax purposes. With $\beta$ in the user cost of housing, one obtains

$$r(k) = [i + \gamma](1 - \beta\tau)P(k).$$

Clearly, $\partial r/\partial\beta = -\tau[1 + \gamma]P(k) < 0$ and $\partial^2 r/\partial k\partial\beta = -\tau[1 + \gamma]P_k > 0$, so that increasing deductibility reduces the user cost of housing, shifting the aftertax housing price curve downward and rotating counterclockwise, making the curve shallower. From chapter 2 it is known that the shift will tend to increase MBD, whereas the rotation tends to reduce MBD; given the offsetting effects of $\beta$ on MBD, the consumer location response can take either sign.

With respect to Muth's (1969) analysis, it is true that the reduction in user cost stimulates housing demand, increasing MBD as in Muth's story, but it also reduces MBD by flattening the housing price function. The net effect on MBD, and hence location demand, cannot be ascertained by theory alone, therefore casting doubt on Muth's earlier conclusion about the income tax feeding the suburbanization process.

Still, more can be said; differentiating Muth's equation:

$$
\begin{aligned}
dk^*/d\beta &= \{-P_k\tau[i + \gamma]x - \tau P_k P(k)[i + \gamma]^2(1 - \beta t)(\partial x/\partial r)\}\lambda/V_{kk} \\
&= -P_k\tau[1 + \gamma]x\{1 + r(k)(\partial x/\partial r)/x\}\lambda/V_{kk} \\
&= -P_k\tau[1 + \gamma]x\{1 + E(x, r)\}\lambda/V_{kk}.
\end{aligned}
$$

Given $|E(x, r)| < 1$ in general, $dk^*/d\beta < 0$ and *the implicit homeowner subsidy created by interest and property tax deductibility increases the demand for CBD proximity.* This is in contrast to Muth's earlier conclusion; instead of feeding the postwar suburbanization process, the income tax treatment of housing costs is found to work in the opposite direction.

### Public-Service Effects

Differentiating Muth's equation (3.15) yields the location effect of a change in public service as

$$
dk^*/dg = r_k(\partial x/\partial g)/J. \tag{3.28}
$$

The sign of (3.28) follows that of $\partial x/\partial g$. The intuition is much like the sales tax case: an increase in g increases (decreases) housing demand at each location when x and g are complements (substitutes), increasing (decreasing) the MBD, hence increasing (decreasing) optimal distance.

The total effect on housing demand, comprising direct and reinforcing location effects, is similarly straightforward:

$$
\begin{aligned}
dx^*/dg &= (\partial x/\partial g) + (\partial X/\partial r)r_k(dk^*/dg) \\
&= (\partial x/\partial g)[1 + (\partial X/\partial r)r_k^2/J],
\end{aligned} \tag{3.29}
$$

and $dx^*/dg$ takes the same sign as $\partial x/\partial g$.

## 3.2 ENDOGENOUS LOCAL FISCAL BEHAVIOR

The preceding analysis assumes that tax rates and service levels are set exogenously and independently of each other (that is, there is no explicit government budget constraint), the prevailing approach in spatial analyses of public-sector effects.[5] This section of the chapter seeks to expand understanding of how the public sector affects housing and location demands by endogenizing the public budget.

The property tax provides the greatest source of own-tax revenues for most local governments in the United States. Therefore, following convention, this study assumes that the local government levies only a property tax. To further simplify, it is assumed that the local government under consideration provides only one service, g, per household. The publicly provided service is a pure public good with constant average production cost.[6] Normalizing the average cost to unity, the total expenditure equals this study's measure of the service provided, g.

The determination of g and $\gamma$ in the local public sector is a complex process that is difficult to model simply. It involves the interaction of various groups of agents and coalitions: the public-sector bureaucracy, politicians holding public office, voters and taxpayers, and government employees. Each group has an interest in outcomes and varying degrees of capacity to affect the outcomes. Much theoretical analysis has focused on each group singly, although more of the recent literature attempts to integrate two or more of the groups as agents interacting in pseudomarkets.[7]

The next subsection presents the simplest representative voter model of local fiscal behavior in the traditional nonspatial perspective. The second subsection then extends the model of the spatial market environment to evaluate the endogenous public-sector effect on location demand theory results derived thus far.

### Median Voter Model

The framework considered here ignores the complex institutional structure of public-sector decision making, reducing the system to pure democracy. Politicians are interested in gaining or staying in power (Downs 1957) or simply responding to voters' wishes. The bureaucracy is compliant as well, following voters' dictates as expressed through public office holders. Further, in this "as if" world of public decision making, voters themselves do not pursue strategic agendas and do indeed vote even when the expected gains of that act are less than incurred costs.

The level of expenditure g is determined democratically by majority rule, and the property tax rate $\gamma$ is simultaneously determined from the budgetary constraint requiring that local government revenues match expenditures. This constraint is taken as given, having been set at the constitutional stage, thus ensuring that one group cannot alter the fiscal structure to place the entire tax burden onto another subset of voters.

If the individual voter's preferences over g are single-peaked, that is, each voter has a unique utility-maximizing $g^0$ such that utility declines continuously for all values farther away from $g^0$, then the equilibrium public-service level is the median $g^0$ of all voters in the population. No other service level can command a majority over all other service levels under majority rule voting. The voter whose optimal g is this median $g^0$ in the jurisdiction is identified as the *median voter*, the decisive voter whose preferences describe the social choice outcome. The social decision process reduces to "as if" reflecting the crucial voter's choices, reducing the complex government fiscal behavior to that of the single representative voter.

The median voter hypothesis, that the group's decisions reflect those of the median voter, is a handy simplification, but is it too simple to explain the public choice mechanism? The empirical evidence is mixed, but does lend support to the median voter hypothesis overall: Inman (1978), McEachern (1978), Holcombe (1980), Gramlich and Rubinfeld (1982), Deno and Mehay (1987), and Turnbull and Djoundourian (1994) present evidence supporting the "as if" proposition in applications like this, whereas Romer and Rosenthal (1979a, b, 1982) and Wyckoff (1988) present evidence for different alternative models but against the median voter result.

## SIMPLE MEDIAN VOTER MODEL

Denote the property tax base for the jurisdiction as B and total intergovernmental aid receipts as A. Total expenditures on the public service are g, so that matching revenues to expenditures requires that the property tax rate $\gamma$ be set as

$$\gamma = (g - A)/iB. \qquad (3.30)$$

Suppose, as in the standard voter model, each voter's location and housing consumption are fixed at k and x. The median voter's local tax is then $\gamma Px$, and the budget constraint becomes

$$I - T(k, I) = (1 + \gamma)Px + y$$

$$I^0 + bA = bg + y \tag{3.31}$$

where $I^0 = I - T(k, I)$ and the voter's tax share is $b = Px/iB$.

The representative voter's optimal $y$ and $g$ (recall $x$ is fixed for the time being) are

$$[g(b, I^0 + bA), y(b, I^0 + bA)]$$

$$\equiv \text{argmax } U(x, y, g) \text{ s.t. (3.31)}. \tag{3.32}$$

In the simple median voter model, local fiscal behavior follows the demand properties of (3.32). The public expenditure level declines with greater median voter tax share (that is, $\partial g/\partial I^0 > 0$ implies $\partial g/\partial b < 0$) and increases with intergovernmental aid ($\partial g/\partial I^0 > 0$ implies $\partial g/\partial A > 0$). Also, the model predicts symmetric income and aid comparative statics, that is, $b(\partial g/\partial I^0) = \partial g/\partial A$.[8]

### ENDOGENOUS HOUSING DEMAND

Now move beyond the traditional model by allowing the voter to select housing optimally. Location is still held constant, and location notation continues to be suppressed.

The voter's problem is

$$\max_{x,y,g} U(x, y, g) \text{ s.t. } I^0 = Px[1 + (g - A)/iB] + y.$$

The Lagrangian is

$$L(x, y, g, \lambda) = U(x, y, g) + \lambda\{I^0 - Px[1 + (g - A)/iB] - y\},$$

and the necessary conditions are

$$\partial L/\partial x = U_x - \lambda\{P[1 + \gamma] - Px(g - A)(dB/dx)/iB^2\} = 0, \tag{3.33}$$

$$\partial L/\partial y = U_y - \lambda = 0, \tag{3.34}$$

$$\partial L/\partial g = U_g - \lambda(Px/iB) = 0, \text{ and} \tag{3.35}$$

$$\partial L/\partial \lambda = I^0 - Px[1 + \gamma] - y = 0. \tag{3.36}$$

Since $B$ is the sum of all $Px/i$ over all voter-residents in the jurisdiction, $dB/dx = P/i$ under Cournot behavior.[9] Thus, the term in braces in (3.33) becomes

$$P[1 + \gamma] - Px(g - A)P/iB^2 = P[1 + \gamma] - (Px/iB)P\gamma$$

$$= P[1 + \gamma(1 - b)],$$

and (3.33) can be rewritten as

$$U_x - \lambda P[1 + \gamma(1 - b)] = 0. \tag{3.37}$$

The term attached to the multiplier is recognizable as the marginal cost of housing (MCH). The MCH comprises two effects on the total housing bill: the greater producer price paid to acquire more housing, $P$, plus the greater tax burden from consuming more housing, $P\gamma(1 - b)$. This last term incorporates two effects itself: first, the increase in x increases $Px$, thus increasing the total tax bill due at given rate $\gamma$; and, second, the increase in x increases $B$, thus decreasing the tax rate needed to support public expenditures of g. Of course, $P\gamma(1 - b) > 0$ (since $b < 1$), and the consumer's total property tax bill rises with more x on net.

Rewriting equation (3.35) using $b = Px/iB$:

$$U_g - \lambda b = 0. \tag{3.38}$$

The voter's demands are the solutions to (3.34), (3.36), (3.37), and (3.38). These optimality conditions have familiar interpretations: equations (3.34) and (3.37), (3.37) and (3.38), and (3.34) and (3.38) together reveal, respectively,

$$MRS_{x,y} = MCH, \tag{3.39}$$

$$MRS_{x,g} = MCH/b, \text{ and} \tag{3.40}$$

$$MRS_{y,g} = 1/b, \tag{3.41}$$

where $MRS_{ij}$ is the marginal rate of substitution between goods i and j and the price of y is 1.

The comparative statics of this model differ from the model in which housing consumption is fixed. To examine the income and intergovernmental grants' comparative statics, totally differentiate the first-order conditions (FOC) and solve for the following using Cramer's Rule:

$$\partial g/\partial A = b(\partial g/\partial I^o) + (\partial G/\partial MCH)(dMCH/dA) > 0, \tag{3.42}$$

where G is the compensated or Hicksian demand. Thus, changes in aid in this model reflect two separate effects, the income effect $b(\partial g/\partial I^o)$ arising from the increase in purchasing power and the new effect $(\partial G/\partial MCH)(dMCH/dA)$ arising from the pure price effect of aid on MCH, hence the voter's choice of g. Because $dMCH/dA = -P(1 - b)/B < 0$ from (3.30) and $MCH = P[1 + \gamma(1 - b)]$, increases in aid reduce MCH, which in turn alters the Hicksian demand for public service. Equation (3.42) shows that

$$\partial g/\partial A \gtreqless b(\partial g/\partial I^o) \quad \text{as} \quad \partial G/\partial MCH \gtreqless 0. \tag{3.43}$$

Intuitively, an increase in aid reduces the MCH. If g and x are Hicksian complements, the lower MCH stimulates greater public service demand by itself, holding purchasing power and welfare constant. In this case, $\partial G/\partial MCH > 0$ and this increase in g reinforces the increase in purchasing power effect of A, hence stimulating a greater marginal public service increase than would a comparable increase in purchasing power or money income alone. Thus, Hicksian complementarity between g and x generates the type of asymmetric income-aid responses often found in the empirical literature.

## Location Choice

Denote the Marshallian demands solving (3.33)–(3.36) as

$$[x(P, I^o, A), y(P, I^o, A), g(P, I^o, A)]. \tag{3.44}$$

Substitute (3.44) into $U(x, y, g)$ to find indirect utility:

$$W(P, I^o, A) = U[x(P, I^oA), y(P, I^o, A), g(P, I^o, A)]. \tag{3.45}$$

The properties of (3.45) are

$$W_I = \lambda; \qquad W_A = \lambda b; \qquad W_P = -\lambda(1 + \gamma)x. \tag{3.46}$$

To demonstrate each, differentiate (3.45) with respect to $I^o$:

$$W_I = U_x(\partial x/\partial I^o) + U_y(\partial y/\partial I) + U_g(\partial g/\partial I^o).$$

Since $U_x = \lambda MCD$, $U_y = \lambda$, and $U_g = \lambda b$ from (3.33)–(3.35), this becomes

$$W_I = \lambda[MCH(\partial x/\partial I^o) + (\partial y/\partial I^o) + b(\partial g/\partial I^o)]. \tag{3.47}$$

Now differentiate the voter's budget constraint (3.36) with respect to income to find

$$1 = MCH(\partial x/\partial I^o) + (\partial y/\partial I^o) + b(\partial g/\partial I^o).$$

Substituting this result for the bracketed term in (3.47) yields $W_I = \lambda$, which is the first property in (3.46). Similar derivations yield the second and third results in (3.46).

Now recall $P(k)$ and $I^o = I - T(k, I)$. Insert into (3.45) and maximize with respect to location. The optimal residence site $k^*$ satisfies the FOC

$$dW/dk = W_p P_k - W_I T_k = 0,$$

so that (3.46) yields the usual form of Muth's equation, modestly modified to include property taxation,

$$-P_k(1 + \gamma)x - T_k = 0, \qquad (3.48)$$

or

$$-r_k x - T_k = 0. \qquad (3.49)$$

The second-order condition (SOC) $d^2W/dk^2 < 0$ is assumed to hold globally so that preferences are single-peaked over g, which generates the median voter outcome. Nonetheless, the SOC implies that $k^*$ is unique.

### HOUSING PRICE FUNCTION

The characteristics of P(k) and r(k) follow immediately by rearranging (3.48) and (3.49): $P_k < 0$ and $r_k < 0$, as in the exogenous government model. Convexity is usually derived from the SOC, but in this case the SOC does not ensure $P_{kk} > 0$ because the spatial variation in g and x leads to spatial variation in $\gamma$ itself. The existence of other nondecisive voters, though, ensures that both $P_{kk} > 0$ and $r_{kk} > 0$, since $\gamma$ and g are exogenous to them.

---

### 3.3 HOUSING POLICIES

The federal, state, and local governments are all deeply involved in the workings of U.S. housing markets. Some of the indirect policies, like the mortgage interest deductibility feature of the federal income tax, have already been addressed. This section looks at a group of more direct intrusions in the housing market, the setting of consumption standards and various subsidy schemes. These are part of the more narrowly defined policies, each targeting specific groups of consumers within specific housing markets. The application here serves to demonstrate how urban household theory is applied to evaluate the housing and location demand impacts of consumption and subsidy policies.

Broadly speaking, housing policies range from modification of private market outcomes, primarily by enforcing building codes and zoning and land-use restrictions, to more direct actions, including grants or subsidies to targeted households or outright provision of public housing. These policies influence both sides of the market, demand

and supply. Since the focus here is on household behavior, I consider only those policies directed at the demand side of the market, disregarding the extensive literature concerning zoning, building and other land-use restrictions.[10]

This discussion draws from and extends some of the subsidy policies examined in Turnbull (1993a). The focus is on the application of urban consumer theory, and what insight it provides into the relationship between the policies and location demand, primarily the extent to which the policies prompt targeted households to congregate more or less intensely in the central city. If the private market and public housing authorities respond to the location demands of subsidized households, how would the urban landscape change?

Carlton and Ferreira (1977) provided some interesting simulation evidence. They examined the effects of various subsidy policies in a market with a given housing stock, generally finding that such policies tend to generate greater concentration of poor and minorities within one housing segment (p. 233). Their analysis is broadly aggregated; housing stock is not highly malleable, though, and location demand effects are not considered at all. Still, their results are suggestive at the very least; their conclusion that "housing gap" and "percent of rent" subsidy schemes with minimum consumption constraints generate similar outcomes might be reasonably taken to imply that the difference between the spatial impacts of the policies is trivial. The explicit location demand approach of this chapter therefore provides a contrast in method and, perhaps what is not surprising, provides starkly different results.

### Minimum Housing Consumption Standards

Consider the effect of housing consumption constraints on consumer behavior, in particular the effect of a minimum housing consumption constraint. The purpose of much housing policy is to increase consumption of the targeted individuals to at least some minimum level. This analysis does not consider how such a constraint is actually imposed or enforced, whether by direct government provision of housing or by restrictions on quantities supplied in the private market.[11] The analysis assumes that consumption constraints are not location-specific; that is, the targeted consumers cannot avoid the minimum consumption standard by merely relocating to another part of the urban area. Although binding on the targeted consumer at some location, the minimum consumption standard need not present a binding constraint at all locations for the consumer in the spatial housing market, because housing demand normally increases with distance from the CBD.

Ignoring taxes and public services, suppose the government sets a minimum housing consumption standard of $x_m$. The household's problem is now to select $x$, $y$, and $k$ to maximize utility subject to the budget constraint that total expenditure on housing, nonhousing, and commuting equal money income and the constraint $x \geq x_m$. Denoting the relevant multipliers $\lambda$ and $\mu$, the Lagrangian is

$$L(x, y, k, \lambda, \mu) = U(x, y) + \lambda[I - T(k, I)$$
$$- P(k)x - y] + \mu[x - x_m].$$

The relevant Kuhn-Tucker conditions are

$$\partial L/\partial x = U_x - \lambda P + \mu = 0, \tag{3.50}$$

$$\partial L/\partial y = U_y - \lambda = 0, \tag{3.51}$$

$$\partial L/\partial k = \lambda[-P_k x - T_k] = 0, \tag{3.52}$$

$$\partial L/\partial \lambda = I - T(k, I) - P(k)x - y = 0, \text{ and} \tag{3.53}$$

$$\partial L/\partial \mu = x - x_m \geq 0; \quad \mu[x - x_m] = 0; \quad \mu \geq 0. \tag{3.54}$$

The complementary slackness condition is (3.54). This condition requires that $\mu = 0$ if the minimum consumption constraint is not binding $(x > x_m)$. In this case, conditions (3.50) and (3.51) together yield the familiar consumption equilibrium condition $MRS_{x,y} = P$. In the event that the constraint is binding, (3.54) reveals $\mu > 0$, so that (3.50) and (3.51) leave the modified consumption condition $MRS_{x,y} = P - \mu/\lambda$. Since $\mu > 0$ and given $\lambda > 0$ from (3.51), this condition requires $MRS_{x,y} < P$; the consumer is willing to trade off more housing for nonhousing consumption than the market rate of trade-off dictates, but is precluded from doing so by the consumption constraint imposed as a matter of policy.

Condition (3.52) reduces to the usual statement of Muth's equation for location equilibrium,

$$-P_k x - T_k = 0. \tag{3.55}$$

This condition obviously remains unaltered by the introduction of the consumption constraint.

There are several possible ways to proceed with the analysis, but the approach taken here appears to be the most straightforward, particularly for the analysis of subsequent subsidy schemes. First, note that the household studied in chapter 2 has $\mu = 0$. Thus, the only case left to consider is the household subject to binding consumption constraint. Focusing on this case, the analysis is considerably simplified by substituting $x = x_m$ and solving the budget constraint for $y$, to restate the problem as the location choice part of the original problem outlined previously, or

$$\max_k U[x_m, I - P(k)x_m - T(k, I)].$$

The selection of the optimal location $k^*$ immediately determines non-housing consumption $y^* = I - P(k^*)x_m - T(k^*, I)$. This location satisfies Muth's equation (3.55) with $x = x_m$:

$$-P_k x_m - T_k = 0. \tag{3.56}$$

By (3.55) or (3.56), $P_k < 0$ for location equilibrium whether or not the consumption constraint is binding. The effect of the constraint on location demand is found by differentiating (3.56) to find

$$dk^*/dx_m = P_k/[-P_{kk}x_m - T_{kk}] > 0. \tag{3.57}$$

The increase in $x_m$ increases the savings on housing expenditures that can be obtained from moving farther out; the higher MBD prods the consumer to locate farther out from the CBD. The minimum consumption policy decreases the demand for CBD proximity by targeted households, providing a force for dispersion farther out in the urban area than the households would otherwise desire. Of course, this policy at the same time reduces consumer welfare ($dU^*/dx_m = dU(x_m, y^*)/dx_m = -\mu < 0$), a result that provides an argument for some sort of housing subsidization scheme to compensate the targeted households for this welfare loss.

Before turning to the simultaneous effect of subsidies, though, it is convenient to address other aspects of the consumption constraint, specifically how the comparative static properties of housing and location demands are altered under constraint. Of course, because housing demand is determined by the constraint when binding, changes in consumer income, tastes, commuting costs, and so forth, will have no effect on housing demand so long as the constraint remains binding. Thus, the discussion concentrates upon location demand exclusively. These results are summarized in table 3.2, along with the comparative statics of the policies examined later.

The effect of income is found from (3.56) under constraint:

$$dk^*/dI = T_{kI}/[-P_{kk}x_m - T_{kk}] \leq 0 \quad \text{as} \quad T_{kI} \geq 0. \tag{3.58}$$

If an increase in wage income increases the marginal time cost of travel, then the consumer reduces commuting distance by moving

Table 3.2  HOUSING POLICY EFFECTS ON CBD-EMPLOYED AND LOCALLY
EMPLOYED HOUSEHOLDS

| Policy or Parameter Change | Sufficient Condition | Location k* |
|---|---|---|
| **Binding Consumption Standard Alone:** | | |
| Minimum consumption constraint | | + |
| Household income | | + |
| Housing price function | $P_{k\alpha} > 0$ | — |
| | $P_{k\alpha} = 0$ | 0 |
| | $P_{k\alpha} < 0$ | + |
| Travel cost function | $T_{k\alpha} > 0$ | — |
| (CBD-employed | $T_{k\alpha} = 0$ | 0 |
| households only) | $T_{k\alpha} < 0$ | + |
| **Subsidy Policies:** | | |
| Ability-to-pay with binding consumption standard | | — |
| Per-unit subsidy with binding consumption standard | | 0 |
| Percentage subsidy: | | |
| No binding consumption constraint | Marshallian demand price elastic | + |
| | Unit elastic | 0 |
| | Price inelastic | — |
| Binding consumption constraint: | | |
| Consumption constraint effect | | + |
| Subsidy effect | | — |

Notes: Policy or parameter changes entail increases in the relevant exogenous terms.
CBD, central business district.

closer to the job site in the CBD. If changes in wage income do not
affect the MCD, then there is no location demand response.

To examine the effect of changes in housing price, employ the shift
parameter $\alpha$, where $P(k, \alpha)$ and $P_\alpha > 0$. Using Muth's equation under
constraint,

$$dk^*/d\alpha = P_{k\alpha}/[-P_{kk}x_m - T_{kk}]. \qquad (3.59)$$

Recalling that the denominator is negative, a level or parallel shift in
the housing price surface across all locations ($P_{k\alpha} = 0$) has no effect
on location demand under the minimum housing consumption policy.

If the price function rotates, though, the story is quite different. A steeper price gradient ($P_{k\alpha} < 0$) increases the MBD by increasing the amount of housing expenditure savings obtainable by moving farther from the CBD, and the consumer resides farther out. On the other hand, a shallower price gradient ($P_{k\alpha} > 0$) decreases the MBD and the consumer resides closer to the CBD.

Although all three price change situations are intuitively appealing in the constrained decision environment, they all contrast sharply with the unconstrained case where $P_{k\alpha} \geq 0$ is sufficient for $dk^*/d\alpha < 0$, whereas $P_{k\alpha} < 0$ leaves the outcome ambiguous. The unconstrained case results are complicated by the response of housing demand to the upward shift in the price surface, since under normality the tendency is for housing demand to decrease. This by itself reduces the MBD, prompting the consumer to decrease distance in the absence of any price function slope effects, as noted previously. The slope effects in the unconstrained model therefore serve to reinforce or offset the effect of the price function shift on MBD, and hence location. In the constrained case examined here, though, the shift in $P(k)$ has no direct effect on MBD because housing demand adjustment is precluded by the constraint.

To finish characterizing the properties of location demand under constraint, introduce the shift parameter into the commuting cost function to examine the effect of travel cost changes, $T(k, \alpha)$, where $T_\alpha > 0$ indicates an increase in commuting cost. As before, implicitly differentiate Muth's equation under constraint to get

$$dk^*/d\alpha = T_{k\alpha}/[-P_{kk}x_m - T_{kk}] \gtreqless 0 \quad \text{as} \quad T_{k\alpha} \gtreqless 0. \quad (3.60)$$

An increase in the MCD gives the consumer an incentive to reside closer to the CBD job site, whereas a decrease in the MCD has the opposite effect. These clear-cut results, too, conflict with the unconstrained case examined in chapter 2. In the unconstrained case, the increase in travel cost reduces net income at all locations, which by itself reduces housing demand and hence MBD. The lower MBD serves to decrease the optimal distance. At the same time, though, the change in the travel cost function may involve an increase or decrease in MCD, which can either reinforce or offset the lower MBD effect on location demand. Of course, in the constrained case examined here, there is no change in MBD because there is no change in housing demand, given the binding nature of the constraint. The total effect of travel cost changes on location demand therefore solely reflects changes in the MCD.

## Housing Subsidy Based on Ability-to-Pay

One important aspect of the preceding housing policy is that a minimum consumption level is stipulated and enforced, but no effort is made to compensate the targeted households for the greater housing costs that must be incurred if such purchases are to be made at the going market rates. More realistically, this section considers one method of subsidizing the consumer to mitigate the utility loss from the consumption constraint; the method involves basing housing outlays on an ability-to-pay or percentage of income basis. Set up this way, total housing expenditures can be held below what must be paid in the market, with the government providing a subsidy to cover the difference between consumer payments and market rents (or, in the case of public housing, production costs).

This policy resembles the usual fee structure encountered in public housing projects in major U.S. cities. It also resembles the "housing gap" or housing voucher method of subsidy in which the monthly housing allowance is stipulated to be a decreasing function of household disposable income (Carlton and Ferreira, Jr. 1977). In the case of public housing, the consumption constraint is imposed by the housing authority; similar constraints can be instituted for housing gap subsidies when recipients are allowed to purchase housing services in the private market by stipulating minimum living area and other characteristics of reimbursable units. Either way, the ability-to-pay method of subsidy is explicitly tied to the fulfillment of the consumption constraint $x_m$.

The household's problem is modified to selecting $y$ and $k$ to maximize utility subject to the budget constraint

$$I - h = y + T(k, I),$$

where $h$ is the lump-sum housing bill levied on the targeted household subject to the policy. Substitute $x_m$ for $x$ in the utility function, solve the new budget constraint for $y$, and substitute that into the utility function to restate the household's problem as

$$\max_k U[x_m, I - h - T(k, I)] \quad \text{s.t.} \quad k \geq 0.$$

The nonnegativity constraint on location turns out to be particularly meaningful here and is therefore explicitly introduced. The optimal location satisfies the Kuhn-Tucker conditions

$$dU/dk = -U_y T_k \leq 0; \quad (dU/dk)k = 0; \quad k \geq 0.$$

Since $U_y T_k > 0$, this set of conditions requires $k^* = 0$: *under the public housing or housing gap scheme, the household's optimal location is as near the CBD as possible.* The MBD is zero for the household whose rent bill is fixed at $h$ by the subsidy policy. The MCD remains positive, though, since the household still commutes to the CBD regularly. It is intuitively appealing that the household will therefore try to minimize the commuting costs by residing as close to the CBD as possible, thereby maximizing the amount of nonhousing consumption.

What we see, then, is that the minimum housing consumption constraint by itself prods the household to increase its commute, whereas the introduction of housing bills based on ability-to-pay overshadows that force, increasing the demand for CBD proximity. The method of housing expenditures subsidy incorporated in the policy clearly enters as an important dimension of the policy when it comes to location demand impacts.

### Subsidy per Unit of Housing

Consider an alternative form of housing subsidy, one based on housing consumption, the per-unit subsidy of $s$. Suppose $[x^0, k^0]$ is the household's optimal choice of housing and location in the absence of a consumption/subsidy policy. If the policymaker wishes to compensate the target consumer for the extra financial burden of acquiring additional housing to meet the consumption constraint, the subsidy is set as $s = P(k^0)[x_m - x^0]/x_m$.

With this per-unit subsidy, the consumer under constraint must pay the housing price difference $P(k) - s$ directly. The consumer's budget constraint with the policy is therefore

$$I = [P(k) - s]x_m + y + T(k, I).$$

Substitute into the utility function with $x_m$ to revise the household's location choice problem,

$$\max_k U[x_m, I - P(k)x_m + sx_m - T(k, I)],$$

where $k^*$ satisfies the usual version of Muth's equation under consumption constraint, equation (3.56). Thus, all of the conclusions for the minimum housing consumption policy without subsidy pertain here as well: the policy with the per-unit subsidy gives the household for whom the $x_m$ constraint is binding an incentive to live farther away from the CBD in the urban area.

Interestingly, it turns out that the per-unit subsidy itself has no effect on location demand for this consumer. Since this form of subsidy is effectively the same as a parallel downward shift in the housing price function, in the unconstrained world of chapter 2 the subsidy would increase housing demand at each distance, thus increasing MBD; the end result is that the household resides farther out in the urban area. Under constraint, though, the lower net price of housing does not alter housing demand, and hence does not affect the MBD or location demand. *The total policy effect on location demand therefore reflects the housing consumption restriction alone.*

The parallels between consumption constraint alone and with per-unit subsidization extend throughout the analysis here. Specifically, all of the previous comparative statics for the constraint-alone case extend to the subsidy case as well.

### Subsidy as Percentage of Housing Expenditure

In the rent-conditioned housing gap subsidy or percentage-of-rent scheme, the targeted consumer receives a subsidy that is $\eta$ percent of housing expenditures.

#### SUBSIDY ALONE

The aid recipient faces the net price of housing equal to $(1 - \eta)P(k)$, and the household budget constraint becomes

$$I = (1 - \eta)P(k)x + y + T(k, I)$$
$$I = r(k)x + y + T(k, I),$$

where $r(k) = (1 - \eta)P(k)$ in the second line. The subsidy shifts the housing price function facing the consumer downward and rotates it counterclockwise, which is the opposite effect of the property tax examined earlier. Drawing from that discussion, the comparative statics for housing demand and location demand are ambiguous a priori. Further, just as the location response to the property tax is seen to depend upon the price elasticity of Marshallian demand in (3.21), a similar condition applies for the percentage subsidy under study here:

$$dk^*/d\eta \gtreqless 0 \quad \text{as} \quad |E(x, r)| \gtreqless 1. \tag{3.61}$$

Notice the reversal of the sign of the elasticity condition in (3.61) relative to (3.21). As in the property tax case, the fact that demand is price inelastic implies a clear location response to changes in the subsidy rate, but in this case the subsidy increases the demand for CBD proximity.

Looking at how the subsidy affects housing demand, as in the property tax case $dx^*/d\eta$, is ambiguous, comprising as it does offsetting direct and location effects of the subsidy scheme.

### SUBSIDY WITH BINDING HOUSING CONSUMPTION CONSTRAINT

Having reviewed the effect of a percentage housing subsidy alone, consider now the combined effects of such a subsidy with the minimum housing consumption policy. Assume a target consumer for whom the consumption constraint is binding. Setting $x = x_m$ throughout and solving the modified budget constraint for $y$, the consumer's problem is restated as

$$\max_k U[x_m, I - (1 - \eta)P(k)x_m - T(k, I)].$$

The optimal location $k^*$ satisfies the FOC

$$U_y[-(1 - \eta)P_k x_m - T_k] = 0,$$

so that Muth's equation is, under subsidy here:

$$-(1 - \eta)P_k x_m - T_k = 0. \tag{3.62}$$

Using (3.62) the policy effects on location demand are as follows:

$$dk^*/dx_m = (1 - \eta)P_k/[-(1 - \eta)P_{kk}x_m - T_{kk}] > 0 \text{ and} \tag{3.63}$$

$$dk^*/d\eta = -P_k x_m/[-(1 - \eta)P_{kk}x_m - T_{kk}] < 0. \tag{3.64}$$

Because an increase in $x_m$ increases MBD, the consumer increases the optimal commute in response to the consumption constraint—just as in the model without subsidy, considered earlier. Interestingly, the subsidy rate effect here differs from the unconstrained subsidy case above. Here the subsidy flattens the net housing price function facing the consumer, the flatter slope lowering MBD, hence prodding the household to reside closer to the CBD. But notice that not only does the percentage subsidy elicit a different response under constraint than without constraint, but it also elicits a different location response than the per-unit subsidy. Recall that the latter leaves optimal location unchanged under consumption constraint. Once again, the specific subsidy scheme chosen is seen to affect the net policy outcome.

Results (3.63) and (3.64) capture the policy effects of each component of the consumption restriction-subsidy policy separately. A relevant question, though, centers upon the combined policy: Will the consumption constraint on the subsidy effect dominate on location demand when they change simultaneously? If the subsidy is set for a particular $x_m$ to give the household sufficient housing aid to purchase the additional housing consumption requirement at the pre-subsidy optimal location $k^0$, then $P(k^0)\eta x_m = P(k^0)[x_m - x^0]$ where $x^0$ is the pre-policy housing demand. Thus,

$$\eta = 1 - x^0/x_m, \tag{3.65}$$

so that a change in the minimum housing consumption constraint requires a concomitant change in the subsidy rate of

$$d\eta/dx_m = x^0/x_m^2. \tag{3.66}$$

The results (3.63) and (3.64) also reveal

$$(1 - \eta)(dk^*/d\eta) = -x_m(dk^*/dx_m), \tag{3.67}$$

so that, substituting (3.65) into (3.67) and rearranging reveals

$$\begin{aligned} dk^*/d\eta &= -(dk^*/dx_m)x_m/[1 - 1 + x^0/x_m] \\ &= -(dk^*/dx_m)(x_m^2/x^0). \end{aligned} \tag{3.68}$$

Now, using (3.65), a change in $x_m$ with subsidy has the net location effect

$$\begin{aligned} \Delta k^*/\Delta x_m &= dk^*/dx_m + (dk^*/d\eta)(d\eta/dx_m) \\ &= dk^*/dx_m - (dk^*/x_m)(x_m^2/x^0)(x^0/x_m^2) \tag{3.69} \\ &= (dk^*/dx_m)[1 - 1] = 0, \end{aligned}$$

using (3.66) and (3.68) for the second equality. What (3.69) establishes is the neutrality of the net consumption-subsidy policy as constructed here: *the household's demand for CBD proximity remains unaffected by simultaneous changes in the consumption constraint and the percentage subsidy policy satisfying (3.65).*

## Locally Employed Housing Subsidy Recipients

Now suppose the housing subsidy recipient is locally employed instead of CBD employed as assumed previously. The local employment sector, comprising residential service industries, is pictured as the most likely outlet for lower-income workers' skills. The analysis of locally employed household behavior under subsidy is therefore particularly relevant.

Recall from chapter 2 that the defining characteristic of the locally employed worker is that he or she does not commute. Like the worker's CBD employed counterpart, though, the worker does face decreasing housing price with distance from the CBD, although his or her consumable income $I(k)$ varies by location due to spatially varying wage rates.

### HOUSING CONSUMPTION CONSTRAINT

Under the local employment assumption, the household's problem is to select $x$, $y$, and residence and work site $k$ to maximize $U(x, y)$ subject to the housing consumption constraint $x \geq x_m$ and $I(k) = P(k)x + y$. As before, the analysis focuses upon the consumer targeted by the housing policy, for whom the constraint is binding. Without subsidies, then, set $x = x_m$ and solve the budget constraint for $y$ and substitute into the utility function to restate the consumer's problem as

$$\max_k U[x_m, I(k) - P(k)x_m].$$

The optimal location $k^*$ satisfies

$$U_y[I_k - P_k x_m] = 0,$$

which reduces to the local employment version of Muth's equation, or

$$-P_k x_m + I_k = 0. \tag{3.70}$$

As in Chapter 2, this condition implies the usual negative wage income gradient. This equation also reveals that the locally employed consumer's location demand responds to the housing consumption policy just like the CBD-employed consumer: $dk^*/dx_m > 0$, and the policy remains a force for greater dispersion of the targeted locally employed population toward the urban periphery.

### PUBLIC HOUSING AND HOUSING GAP SUBSIDIES

For the CBD-employed aid recipient, the public housing and housing gap schemes were essentially lump-sum rent payment schemes based on ability-to-pay; regardless of where the consumer locates, he or she earns the same wage income and pays the same bill for housing. For the locally employed aid recipient, though, basing rent payments on ability-to-pay means that relocating farther away from the CBD reduces the housing bill—because the measured ability-to-pay (income) falls with distance. It seems reasonable to expect this spatial variation in rent bill to alter the locally employed household's behavior.

Define $v$ as the percentage of income to be paid as rent to receive the housing services $x_m$; the relevant budget constraint is now

$$I(k)(1 - v) = y.$$

Substituting into the utility function, the household's problem is modified to

$$\max_k U[x_m, I(k)(1 - v)] \quad \text{s.t.} \quad k \geq 0.$$

I again explicitly draw out the nonnegativity condition on distance. The optimal location satisfies the Kuhn-Tucker conditions

$$dU/dk = U_y I_k (1 - v) \leq 0; \quad (dU/dk)k = 0; \quad k \geq 0. \quad (3.71)$$

Notice that location equilibrium no longer requires the negative wage income gradient. If the gradient is negative, though, (3.71) requires $k^* = 0$, with the resulting situation like the CBD employment case, where the household has incentive to live at the highest wage site possible, as close to the CBD as possible.

### Per-Unit and Ad Valorem Subsidies

The CBD and local employment cases yield identical results for these types of subsidies. As summarized in table 3.2, per-unit subsidies, when granted simultaneously with the imposition of binding housing consumption constraint, have no effect on location demand, whereas ad valorem subsidies increase the demand for CBD proximity.

---

### 3.4 CONCLUDING REMARKS

This chapter integrated the public sector into the consumer housing and location demand model. It showed how the qualitative housing price and demand-location characteristics remain unaltered by the introduction of a taxing and service-providing public sector. Adding endogenous housing and location choice to the simple median voter model did, however, fundamentally alter the comparative static predictions of the voter model, in particular, inducing asymmetric income-intergovernmental grants effects on public spending.

This chapter also considered the relation between housing policies and location demand, looking at both the CBD and locally employed household cases. What is surprising is that the subsidy policies are identical for both types of consumers. Minimum consumption standards by themselves decrease the demand for CBD proximity and increase the demand for outlying sites when imposed without a subsidy. The subsidy scheme, however, turns out to be the critical linchpin in the integrated housing policy; when applied in conjunction with housing subsidies, the consumption constraint effect on location demand varies by type of subsidy.

Similarly, the effects of housing subsidies hinge critically upon whether or not they accompany consumption restrictions. As part of an integrated housing policy, subsidies based on ability-to-pay increase the demand for CBD proximity, whereas per-unit subsides do not affect the consumer's location demand. Percentage-of-rent or ad valorem subsidies increase the demand for CBD proximity, but not as much as the ability-to-pay subsidy.

Taxes and housing policies affect the spatial configuration of urban areas, and therefore need to be formally integrated into planning frameworks dealing with regional development patterns. Spatial housing demand patterns vary with the type of policy adopted, something to consider when periodically revising tax and housing policies. For example, shifts from public housing wherein tenants' rents are based upon ability-to-pay to stronger reliance on housing vouchers or rent coupons will alter spatial patterns of housing demand by targeted groups; to the extent that the private market is allowed to accommodate these location demand changes, such policy shifts by themselves may generate migration of stably employed but low-income households from central cities to the urban fringe, reinforcing the pervasive U.S. suburbanization pattern of the postwar period.

A deficiency of the modeling effort in this chapter is its formal neglect of involuntary unemployment among urban households. This aspect, at least for temporary or uncertain unemployment, can be dealt with directly, as the analysis in chapter 5 illustrates. Nonetheless, for those permanently unemployed, there appears to be no budgetary or time penalty to living on the urban fringe where housing price is at its lowest in the static model. Without the CBD orientation, what drives the propensity for the interior location of these households, whether receiving housing aid or not? And how will the various subsidy schemes alter observed outcomes for this group of urban poor? Dynamic filtering of older housing in urban area interiors, nonmarket constraints on low-income housing sites, and other structural and political factors are all good candidates for further consideration.

## Notes

1. See applications by Polinsky and Rubinfeld (1978), Sullivan (1985), and Wildasin (1985). Also note that partial equilibrium analysis provides insights perhaps obscured, but not likely overridden, at the market level of aggregation. For example, if an increase in a publicly provided service is found to decrease the demand for CBD proximity, it would be surprising to find, upon aggregation, that the new market-level equilibrium lowers interior housing prices enough to actually increase the overall demand for CBD proximity.

2. This is the case when the local income tax is "piggybacked" on the federal tax, which allows interest deductibility. The implicit interest cost is, of course, not deductible in the federal IRS Code, but for simplicity the entire interest cost is assumed deductible in (3.2). If the property tax is not deductible for income tax purposes, then (3.2) becomes $r = [i(1 - \tau) + \rho]R$. See Blackley and Follain (1983) for explicit treatment of the interaction of income tax with the inflation premium in the user cost, a complication ignored here.

3. If sales taxes were deductible for income tax purposes, then the effective sales tax rate would be $\delta(1 - \tau)$ and (3.5) would become

$$I(1 - \tau) = P(k)(1 - \tau)(1 + \gamma)x + [1 + \delta(1 - \tau)]y + T[k, I(1 - \tau)],$$

so that, contrary to what one might anticipate, even in this case with complete deductibility the income tax will not be neutral.

4. Note that the condition is *Marshallian complementarity*, not *Hicksian complementarity*. In the two good models, both must be Hicksian substitutes, but may be Marshallian substitutes or complements.

5. See Polinsky and Rubinfeld (1978), Haurin (1981), Sullivan (1985), Wildasin (1985), and Turnbull (1989), for models with an exogenous public sector, with and without a budget constraint.

6. This is a simplification. Most local public goods are not pure public goods, but exhibit congestion or rivalrousness in consumption. Local public goods may also exhibit a spatial consumption dimension not captured here (Hochman 1982).

7. See Mueller (1989) for an excellent survey of the literature. See Niskanen (1971) for analysis of bureaucratic behavior and Downs (1957) for politician-voter models.

8. Empirical evidence does not strongly support this symmetric income-aid comparative static result. Instead, we tend to observe the so-called flypaper effect, that aid is more stimulative than income on public spending (Gramlich 1970). There are several explanations for the observed asymmetry: voting agenda control by public sector officeholders (Romer and Rosenthal 1980); the effects of pressure groups (Dougan and Kenyon 1988); the effects of taxable capital mobility (Turnbull and Niho 1986); fiscal illusion (Oates 1979; Turnbull 1992a); and statistical bias (Megdal 1987). See Fisher (1982) for additional discussion.

9. Under Cournot behavior, the median voter assumes all other consumers do not change their housing consumption as g and $\gamma$ change. Daugherty (1985) shows that Cournot behavior ensures rational economic equilibria in static models like this one.

10. See Fischel (1990) for a summary of the empirical literature.

11. Even though "housing services" are difficult to measure in practice, proxies like square footage per occupant, specifications for functioning heating or cooling, plumbing, storm windows and screens on windows, structural integrity, and so on, are imposed for both general populations as well as for those individuals targeted for the subsidy policies added to the model in subsequent sections of this chapter.

# Chapter Four

# UNCERTAINTY ANALYSIS

Chapters 2 and 3 examined urban household behavior under certainty, where all relevant economic variables take known nonstochastic values at the time consumption decisions are made. Chapters 4 and 5 relax the certainty assumption, addressing urban consumer behavior under conditions of uncertainty. The justification for this extension of the model lies in the peculiar nature of housing consumption itself. Housing capital represents a durable good whose output is difficult to adjust within the very short term. As a result, consumers cannot readily adapt housing or residence location to changes in employment status, income, user price of housing, housing quality, or even neighborhood externalities, especially when the duration of such changes is shorter than the consumption period for housing. In such situations consumers face uncertain incomes or housing prices, and so on, over the consumption period; the analysis of consumer behavior under uncertainty simply recognizes this possibility and focuses upon how the introduction of the various sources of risk affect model predictions. This chapter brings together various elements of uncertainty theory in preparation for the extended housing and location demand analysis in chapter 5. As such, it summarizes the method of consumer uncertainty theory and introduces recent results that are critical to understanding and extending the subsequent analysis.

## 4.1 SINGLE VARIABLE EXPECTED UTILITY FUNCTION

In the certainty theory of consumer behavior, preferences are defined over bundles of goods $v = [x\ y]$. In uncertainty theory, though, the point of departure is different; consumer preferences are defined over *uncertain prospects* or bundles of uncertain outcomes, rather than bundles of goods themselves. To be more specific about just what uncertain prospects entail, begin by assuming that the consumer is concerned not with bundles of consumable goods but, rather, with a single composite good, say wealth, $W$. Given that various wealth levels $\theta_1, \ldots, \theta_n$ might be realized with respective probabilities $\pi_1, \ldots, \pi_n$ (where $\Sigma_i \pi_i = 1$), the bundle $A = [\ldots \theta_i \ldots; \ldots \pi_i \ldots]$ represents an uncertain prospect. Similarly, one can present another uncertain prospect, $A'$, wherein elements of the wealth-outcomes vector and/or elements of the probability vector may differ from those constituting uncertain bundle $A$. For what follows, consumer preferences are established over all possible uncertain prospects, much like consumer preferences are defined over all possible consumption bundles in the certainty model.

## Expected Utility Theorem

The importance of von Neumann and Morganstern's (1947) seminal work on decision making under uncertainty is that simple assumptions are sufficient to establish the expected utility ($EU$) function over uncertain prospects,

$$EU(A) = \sum_i \pi_i U(\theta_i).$$

Like the neoclassical utility function under certainty, this expected utility function is (1) order-preserving, that is, $EU(A) > EU(A')$ iff $APA'$, $EU(A) = EU(A')$ iff $AIA'$, etc., (2) continuous, and (3) unique up to a linear transformation, in the sense that if $EU$ is a legitimate expected utility function then so is $EV = a + bEU$ ($a \geq 0, b > 0$).

The adaptation of the expected utility function to a continuously distributed stochastic term $\theta$, where $F(\theta)$ represents the distribution function, is straightforward:

$$EU(\theta) = \int_{\underline{\theta}}^{\overline{\theta}} U(\theta) dF(\theta),$$

where the limits of integration are the support of $\theta$.

## Attitudes toward Risk

Consider an uncertain prospect, $A$, whose expected value is

$$\mu = \sum_i \pi_i \theta_i.$$

A risk-averse individual, when confronted with the choice of $A$ or its actuarially fair outcome, $\mu$, with certainty, will select the certain outcome, or $EU(\theta) < U(\mu)$. There is a connection between risk aversion and the shape of the expected utility function, with $EU(\theta) < U(\mu)$ when $U'' < 0$. The consumer is risk averse when $U'' < 0$, that is, when $U(\theta)$ is strictly concave.

## Measures of Risk Aversion

Using the direct tie between the second derivative $U''$ and risk aversion, the task is now to provide some measure of the degree or strength of risk aversion. There are several popular risk-aversion measures. The Arrow-Pratt Measure of Absolute Risk Aversion is $R^A = -U''/U'$.

To understand Pratt's (1964) justification for this risk-aversion index, I introduce the notion of *risk premium* as the maximum amount the risk-averse consumer will be willing to pay to obtain the certain outcome $W$ over the uncertain bundle $A$. Suppose bundle $A$ comprises elements $[W + \theta]$, where $\theta$ is stochastic with $E[\theta] = 0$ and finite variance $VAR(\theta) > 0$. Defined this way, the risk premium $\rho$ satisfies

$$U(W - \rho) = EU(W + \theta). \tag{4.1}$$

Expanding both sides of (4.1) around $W$:

$$U(W) - \rho U'(W) = E[U(W) + \theta U'(W) + (1/2)\theta^2 U''(W)],$$

so that, using $E[\theta] = 0$ and $E[\theta^2] = VAR(\theta)$, one obtains $\rho U'(W) = -(1/2)VAR(\theta)U''(W)$. Thus,

$$\rho = (1/2)VAR(\theta)[-U''/U'] = (1/2)VAR(\theta)R^A, \tag{4.2}$$

using the preceding risk index definition. As risk aversion rises (holding the overall level of $\theta$ riskiness, measured by $VAR[\theta]$, constant), the risk premium $\rho$ rises, and by (4.2) so must $R^A$. Thus, argues Pratt, $R^A$ provides an appropriate index of risk aversion.

The Arrow-Pratt Measure of Relative Risk Aversion is $R^R = -\theta U''/U'$. Pratt's (1964) justification for the relative risk-aversion index $R^R$, not surprisingly, is similar. Given $\theta$ riskiness (i.e., $VAR[\theta]$), greater risk aversion translates into a higher risk premium, and the higher risk premium translates into a greater risk index $R^R$ as well. Another measure of risk aversion is the Index of Partial Relative Risk Aversion (PRRA), or $R^P = -\theta U''(W + \theta)/U'(W + \theta)$, where $W$ is nonstochastic and $\theta$ is stochastic (Menezes and Hanson 1970).

Arrow (1970) argued that we would intuitively expect a risk-averse agent to be willing to pay a lower (or at least not higher) risk premium when wealth rises but risk remains unchanged. Since $R^A$ varies with the risk premium, this implies constant absolute risk aversion (CARA) or decreasing absolute risk aversion (DARA)—popular assumptions in applied economic analysis. Similar arguments justify increasing relative risk aversion (IRRA) and increasing partial relative risk aversion (IPRRA) as other popular assumptions for applied analysis.

---

*4.2 INVESTMENT PORTFOLIO MODEL*

Before proceeding to the more complicated two-argument utility function, it is useful to present a simple application. The example used in this section is based on Arrow (1970).

**The Model**

Consider an investor with initial wealth $W$. The investor can either invest in an asset $y$ with riskless rate of return $r$, or invest in an asset $x$ with risky (stochastic) rate of return $\theta$. The risky rate of return need not be positive in all states for what follows; that is, the risky investment may realize a loss. Nonetheless, the investor knows the probability distribution of $\theta$.

The investor must decide how much wealth to put into the risky endeavor, and the remainder is invested in the riskless asset. If the investor selects risky investment $x$, his or her portfolio evolves according to

$$\omega = (1 + r)y + (1 + \theta)x. \qquad (4.3)$$

Clearly $\omega$ is stochastic because $\theta$ is random, and has variance $\text{VAR}(\omega)$ $= x^2 \text{VAR}(\theta)$.

Formally, the investor's problem is

$$\max_{x,y} EU(\omega) = EU[(1 + r)y + (1 + \theta)x] \text{ s.t. } y + x = W. \qquad (4.4)$$

An interior solution $(x, y > 0)$ shall be assumed throughout.[1]

Solve the constraint in (4.4) for $y = W - x$ and substitute into the objective function; the problem is revised as

$$\max_x EU[(1 + r)(W - x) + (1 + \theta)x]. \qquad (4.5)$$

The optimal risky investment satisfies the necessary condition $dEU(\omega)/dx = 0$, which reduces to

$$E[U'(\omega)(\theta - r)] = 0. \qquad (4.6)$$

The relevant second-order condition (SOC) for a maximum is $E[U''(\omega)(\theta - r)^2] < 0$. Notice that $(\theta - r)^2 > 0$ for $\theta \neq r$, so that risk aversion ensures that the SOC for a proper maximum is satisfied.

Applying the implicit function theorem, solve (4.6) for the optimal risky investment

$$x^* = x(W, r, \sigma, \mu), \tag{4.7}$$

where $\sigma$ is a parameter capturing the degree of $\theta$-riskiness, as explained in detail below, and $E[\theta] = \mu$.

## Comparative Static Analysis

The assumptions about the degree of risk aversion play key roles in uncertainty analysis. Arrow (1970), for example, showed that either *CARA or DARA is sufficient for risky investment to rise with investor wealth and for risky investment to rise with the expected return to the risky asset.* The intuition for the wealth comparative static prediction is straightforward. Under DARA the level of investor risk aversion decreases as wealth increases, so that the investor is willing to assume greater risk, increasing x as W rises.

Now consider how the investor's behavior changes in response to a change in uncertainty. Recall that the riskiness of $\theta$, hence $\omega$, is tied to the variance of possible outcomes. Roughly, greater uncertainty is tied to greater variance of possible outcomes, holding the expected outcome unchanged. To find the effect of changes in VAR($\theta$) alone, holding $\mu$ constant, a mean preserving spread (mps) is examined as follows. Define the nonstochastic uncertainty parameter $\sigma$ such that $\theta \equiv \mu + \sigma\epsilon$. Since $E[\mu + \sigma\epsilon] = \mu$ and VAR($\mu + \sigma\epsilon$) = $\sigma^2$VAR($\epsilon$), d$\sigma$ > 0 (d$\sigma$ < 0) evaluated at $\sigma = 1$ yields an increase (decrease) in mps, reflecting a greater (lower) level of uncertainty over $\theta$.

Ex post wealth is $\omega = (1 + r)y + (1 + \theta)x$, so that expected wealth is $E[\omega] = (1 + r)y + (1 + \mu)x$, whereas VAR($\omega$) = $\sigma^2 x^2$VAR($\epsilon$). Changes in the uncertainty parameter $\sigma$ leave expected ex post wealth unaffected (for given portfolio), while increasing its variance [dVAR($\omega$)/d$\sigma$ = $2x^2\sigma$VAR($\epsilon$) > 0]. Figure 4.1 depicts the wealth riskiness curve $\pi^1$, the relationship between VAR($\omega$) and x when $\sigma = 1$. This curve depicts the level of wealth riskiness that must be assumed by the investor wishing to invest x in the risky asset. Also shown is the optimal risky investment level, $x^*$, for the initial uncertainty level $\sigma = 1$.

Now suppose uncertainty over the risky rate of return increases. Assuming the expected return remains unchanged, the aim is to find

Figure 4.1  RISK SUBSTITUTION AND RISK-INCOME EFFECTS OF UNCERTAINTY

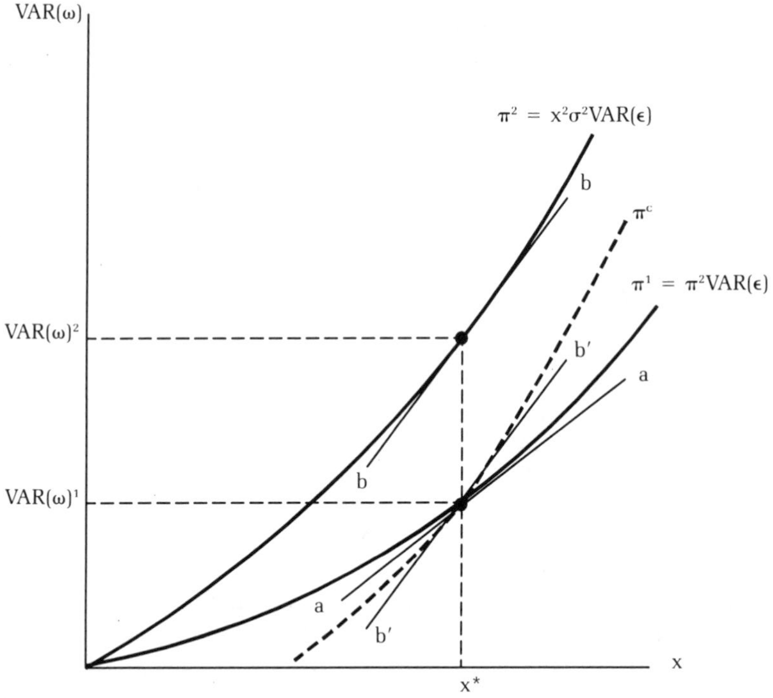

the effect of an increase in mps. In figure 4.1, the new wealth riskiness curve $\pi^2$ pertains to the greater uncertainty case ($\sigma > 1$). Clearly, two things happen to the wealth riskiness curve when $\sigma$ rises from the initial value of unity; the wealth risk curve shifts upward for positive values of $x$ and rotates counterclockwise, becoming steeper at every point. Regarding the latter effect first, note that the slope of $\pi$ is the marginal risk cost of $x$, the increase in wealth risk arising from an increase in risky asset investment. As $\sigma$ rises, the marginal risk cost of $x$ also rises; at the original optimum $x^*$, the marginal risk cost of $x$ is the slope of tangent $aa$, while the marginal risk cost rises to the slope of tangent $bb$ at $x^*$ when $\sigma > 1$. At the same time, though, the upward shift in $\pi$ increases the level of wealth risk at each $x$ (including $x^*$); in terms of the diagram, the *level* of wealth risk rises from $VAR(\omega)^1$ to $VAR(\omega)^2$ at $x^*$.

Figure 4.1 reveals how the separate slope and level effects can be shown to comprise the total change in riskiness. At $x^*$, the riskiness rises by $x^*VAR(\epsilon)$ for $\sigma > 1$. Subtracting this increment in wealth riskiness from the new wealth risk curve $\pi^2$ yields the *compensated wealth riskiness curve* $\pi^c = [\sigma^2 x^2 - x^{*2}]\text{VAR}(\epsilon)$. By construction, this compensated curve has the same slope as the new wealth riskiness curve $\pi^2$. Hence, the compensated curve exhibits a steeper slope $(b'b')$ at $x^*$ than the original curve $(aa)$. The difference in slopes from $aa$ to $b'b'$ measures the increase in the marginal risk cost of $x$ at $x^*$, holding the level of wealth riskiness unchanged at $\text{VAR}(\omega)^1$. The greater marginal risk cost of $x$ by itself prods the consumer to reduce his or her portfolio allocation to the risky asset. This is the *risk substitution effect* of the increase in mean preserving spread $(d\sigma > 0)$.

Having deduced the substitution effect, one can easily see that what remains is to deduce how the investor reacts to the increase in the *level* of wealth riskiness at $x^*$ (and each $x$), that is, the investor's response to an upward shift in the wealth riskiness curve from the compensated $\pi^c$ to the new $\pi^2$. The investor's response to this shift is the *risk income effect* of the increase in mps $(d\sigma > 0)$. Whether the individual increases or decreases $x$ as the risk income effect will in general depend upon his or her risk-aversion characteristics. Under *risk normality*, the greater level of risk will by itself induce the investor to reduce $x$, thus reinforcing the risk substitution effect, leaving $\partial x^*/\partial\sigma < 0$. Under *risk inferiority*, though, the individual responds to the greater level of risk by increasing $x$, thus offsetting the risk substitution effect, leaving $\partial x^*/\partial\sigma$ ambiguous.

With an intuitive understanding of the forces underlying the investor's response to uncertainty, I can now proceed to the formal analysis of outcomes. Substituting $\mu + \sigma\epsilon$ for $\theta$ in (4.6) and differentiating with respect to $\sigma$, evaluating the resultant expression at $\sigma = 1$, leaves the mps comparative static result

$$\partial x^*/\partial\sigma = -E[U'(\omega)\epsilon]/E[U''(\omega)(\theta - r)^2]$$
$$+ xE[U''(\omega)(\theta - r)\epsilon]/E[U''(\omega)(\theta - r)^2]. \quad (4.8)$$

The first term in this equation captures the risk substitution effect, while the second term captures the risk income effect. Since $E[U'\epsilon] = \text{COV}[U', \epsilon]$, which in turn takes the sign of $U''$, risk-aversion implies that the risk substitution effect is negative; as in the previous intuitive discussion, an increase in the marginal risk cost of $x$ holding the level of wealth risk constant prods the individual to shift investment from the risky asset to the riskless asset.

The second term, the risk income effect, cannot be signed from risk aversion alone and therefore requires more analysis. From (4.8), the risk income effect takes the sign of

$$-E[U''(\omega)(\theta - r)\epsilon] = -E[U''(\omega)(\mu + \epsilon - r)\epsilon]$$

$$= -(\mu - r)E[U''(\omega)\epsilon] - E[U''(\omega)\epsilon^2] \quad (4.9)$$

$$= -(\mu - r)COV[U'', \epsilon] - E[U''(\omega)\epsilon^2].$$

The second term is clearly positive under risk aversion. For the first term, though, recall $\mu - r > 0$ for an interior equilibrium, whereas the covariance term takes the sign of $U'''$, the latter of which is positive under CARA or DARA.[2] Thus, the first term is negative, and (4.9) and the risk income effect in (4.8) are ambiguous under CARA or DARA. Nonetheless, the risky investment can be categorized as risk normal (inferior) when the income effect is negative (positive), providing a reinforcing (offsetting) effect to the risk substitution effect.

### Portfolio Investment and Housing Demand

How does this investment portfolio model relate to housing demand? There is no consumption motive for acquiring either asset $x$ or $y$ in the model; thus, the results may be viewed as revealing the individual's "pure" investment motive. If the appreciation rate for housing assets is uncertain ex ante, then the consumer's demand for risky investment captures this pure investment motive for acquiring housing assets in the individual's investment portfolio. Under this interpretation, the pure investment demand for housing increases with wealth under DARA, increases with greater expected rates of return to housing investment under wealth neutrality or normality, and decreases with increased riskiness of housing rate of return under what I have called risk income normality.

Like other consumer durables, housing also has a consumption component. Henderson and Ioannides (1983) recognized this component in addition to the pure investment component by using a standard neoclassical utility function $U(x, y)$ to capture the consumption motive, and the expected utility $E[\phi(\omega)]$ to capture the investment motive. In terms of the notation here, consumer utility is defined as the sum $V(x, y) = U(x, y) + E[\phi(\omega)]$. Setting up the consumption budget constraint and the evolution of ex post wealth (that is, future consumption) reflecting the initial housing investment, this approach can be utilized to integrate both motives for housing demand. To do so, however, is somewhat cumbersome, especially since a more direct method exists, as shown in the section following.

---

## 4.3 CONSUMER CHOICE UNDER INCOME UNCERTAINTY

Moving from the single-argument expected utility function to the two-argument function is not difficult conceptually, but it does raise additional technical problems. Some development of the theory in the context of specific nonspatial applications to savings and labor supply decision appears in Leland (1968), Sandmo (1970), Block and Heineke (1973), and DeSalvo and Eeckhoudt (1982). Nonetheless, recent papers by Dardanoni (1988), Davis (1989), Turnbull (1991), and Turnbull, Glascock, and Sirmans (1991) provide key theoretical results needed to make the two-argument expected utility function model operational in the location demand context. Because the purpose of this chapter is to establish specific results necessary for the spatial analysis of chapter 5, I consider each relevant type of uncertainty in turn: income, price of x, and quality of x. The analysis throughout the remainder of the chapter assumes that housing is selected ex ante, before the realization of the stochastic term. In the general parlance of the uncertainty literature, x (housing) is the certain good and y (all other consumption) is the risky good under income and price risk, while x is the risky good and y is the certain good under quality risk; these distinctions become clear in what follows.

### Model of Income Risk

The consumer's problem is to select housing consumption (x) and nonhousing consumption (y) to maximize expected utility of consumption, $E[U(x, y)]$, subject to an uncertain budget constraint. The utility function $U(x, y)$ is assumed to be strictly concave, reflecting consumer risk aversion.

To begin, assume that household income is uncertain: $I + \theta$ where $I$ is known with certainty and $\theta$ is stochastic, distributed with zero mean and positive variance, $VAR(\theta)$. Once chosen, housing consumption is difficult to adjust in the short run in response to short-run variations in income (i.e., realizations of $\theta$). The household therefore selects x ex ante, to maximize expected utility subject to the ex post budget constraint that spending on x, (that is, Px) plus spending on y (the price of y is unity) equals realized income, $I + \theta$.

$$y = I + \theta - Px \tag{4.10}$$

Expected nonhousing consumption equals planned consumption, $E[y] = I - Px$, and the variance of y is $VAR(y) = VAR(\theta)$. This is therefore an additive risk model (Dardanoni 1988); changes in the ex ante choice variable, x, have no marginal risk cost. In keeping with my earlier discussion of the single variable expected utility function, changes in income uncertainty will invariably generate level risk (risk income) effects with no attendant marginal risk cost (risk price) effects.

Substitute (4.10) into $E[U(x, y)]$ to obtain the consumer problem under income uncertainty:

$$\max_x E[U(x, I + \theta - Px)]. \qquad (4.11)$$

Using the parameter $\sigma$ to designate the level of income uncertainty, the Marshallian demand for housing is a function of price, expected income, and income riskiness, or $x(P, I, \sigma)$ under uncertainty, which is the implicit solution to the following first-order condition (FOC) for problem (4.11),

$$E[U_x] - PE[U_y] = 0. \qquad (4.12)$$

In the theory of demand under certainty, key results concerning the properties of Marshallian and Hicksian demand functions can be most easily derived once some fundamental duality relationships are shown to hold (e.g., Cook 1972). This discussion therefore begins with the extension of demand duality to the income uncertainty environment, integrating some of the main results of Turnbull et al. (1991).

The ordinary or Marshallian housing demand is $x(P, I, \sigma)$, the solution to problem (4.11) as explained previously. Notice that *planned* (rather than realized) nonhousing demand is denoted $m = E[y] = I - Px$. At the consumer's optimum, planned housing and nonhousing consumption, $x(P, I, \sigma)$ and $m(P, I, \sigma)$, respectively, satisfy (4.12) and

$$I = Px(P, I, \sigma) + m(P, I, \sigma), \qquad (4.13)$$

yielding expected utility at the optimum

$$E[U^*] = E[U(x(P, I, \sigma), m(P, I, \sigma) + \theta)], \qquad (4.14)$$

because realized nonhousing consumption is $y = m(P, I, \sigma) + \theta$ by construction. It is important for what follows to note that the concavity of the expected utility function, the objective function in (4.11), ensures that $x(P, I, \sigma)$ and $m(P, I, \sigma)$ are the unique values satisfying (4.12)–(4.14).

The Hicksian or compensated demands for housing and *planned* nonhousing consumption under income uncertainty are the optimal solutions to the problem of finding the planned consumption x and m that incurs the lowest expected expenditure allowing the consumer to attain some expected utility level $E[U]$. Since the expected expenditure is $Px + m$, these Hicksian demand functions are

$\{X(P, E[U], \sigma), M(P, E[U], \sigma)\}$

$$\equiv \text{argmin } Px + m \text{ s.t. } E[U^*] = E[U(x, m + \theta)], \quad (4.15)$$

where the convention of upper-case notation is retained, indicating compensated demands. The concavity of the expected utility function and the linearity of the objective function ensure that $X$ and $M$ in (4.15) are the unique solutions to the FOC:

$$P - \lambda E[U_x] = 0, \quad (4.16)$$

$$1 - \lambda E[U_y] = 0, \text{ and} \quad (4.17)$$

$$E[U] - E[U(x, m + \theta)] = 0. \quad (4.18)$$

The optimum expected expenditure, $\Omega(P, E[U], \sigma)$, is the value of the expected expenditure function, which is in turn defined by substituting (4.15) into the objective function, just as one would under certainty:

$$\Omega(P, E[U], \sigma) = PX(P, E[U], \sigma) + M(P, E[U], \sigma) = I \quad (4.19)$$

Having defined the ordinary and compensated demands, the following demand duality results.

1. *Demand duality.* For expected utility level $E[U^*]$ defined by the solution to problem (4.11)—that is, (4.14)—the result is

$$x(P, I, \sigma) \equiv x(P, \Omega(P, E[U^*], \sigma), \sigma) \equiv X(P, E[U^*], \sigma). \quad (4.20)$$

*Proof.* It is easy to show this important result. Equations (4.16) and (4.17) reduce to

$$E[U_x] - PE[U_y] = 0. \quad (4.21)$$

$X$ and $M$ therefore satisfy (4.18) and (4.21) with $E[U^*]$. Notice, though, that (4.18) and (4.21) with $E[U^*]$ are identical to the conditions defining $x(P, I, \sigma)$ and $m(P, I, \sigma)$, specifically (4.12) and (4.14). Thus, the unique solution to (4.18) and (4.21) also satisfies (4.12) and (4.14) so that $x \equiv X$ and $m \equiv M$ here, as stated by (4.20).

2. *Substitution Theorem.* The effect of own price on Hicksian housing demand is negative under income uncertainty: $\partial X/\partial P < 0$.

*Proof.* Totally differentiate the FOC (4.16)–(4.18) and solve for the comparative static result using Cramer's Rule to find $\partial X/\partial P = E[U_y]/J < 0$, where the bordered Hessian determinant $J < 0$ from the SOC.

Differentiating (4.18) with respect to housing price yields

$$\partial x/\partial P + (\partial x/\partial I)(\partial \Omega/\partial P) = \partial X/\partial P,$$

$$\partial x/\partial P + (\partial x/\partial I)X = \partial X/\partial P,$$

$$\partial x/\partial P + (\partial x/\partial I)x = \partial X/\partial P, \text{ and}$$

$$\partial x/\partial P = \partial X/\partial P - x(\partial x/\partial I), \tag{4.22}$$

where the second line follows with application of $(\partial \Omega/\partial P) = X$ to (4.19) and the third by property 2, above. Simple rearrangement yields (4.22), the analogue to the well-known Slutsky equation under certainty.

3. *Slutsky equation.* The own-price effect on Marshallian housing demand satisfies the Slutsky equation (4.22) under income uncertainty.

In sum, the general properties of housing demand under certainty extend to the income uncertainty environment as well. Similar results, as summarized in subsequent sections, can be shown to hold for housing price uncertainty and housing quality uncertainty cases.

**Income Risk Effects**

I now consider the last set of results that will be useful in the location demand analysis under income uncertainty formally addressed in chapter 5. I am particularly interested in the characterization of the effect of income uncertainty, indexed by $\sigma$, on housing demand, $\partial x/\partial \sigma$.

Recall that $x(P, I, \sigma)$ satisfies (4.12). I wish to analyze the effect of a change in income uncertainty alone, that is, a change in mean preserving spread of the distribution of realizable income values. Substitute the term $\sigma\theta$ for $\theta$ in (4.12). Notice that expected income remains unaltered by changes in $\sigma$ (evaluated at $\sigma = 1$), whereas the variance of income rises and falls with increases and decreases in $\sigma$. Making the substitution into (4.12) and differentiating with respect to $\sigma$, evaluating the outcome at $\sigma = 1$, yields the following income risk effect:

$$\partial x/\partial \sigma = E[U_{xy}\theta - P(k)U_{yy}\theta]/(-D)$$

$$= E[U_{xy} - P(k)U_{yy}]E[\theta]/(-D) \tag{4.23}$$
$$\quad + \text{COV}[U_{xy} - P(k)U_{yy}, \theta]/(-D)$$

$$= \text{COV}[U_{xy} - P(k)U_{yy}, \theta]/(-D),$$

using $E[\theta] = 0$ and $D = E[U_{xx}] + P^2 E[U_{yy}] - 2PE[U_{xy}] < 0$ by the SOC. The properties of similar/dissimilar orderings imply that the covariance term will take the same sign as

$$\partial[U_{xy} - PU_{yy}]/\partial\theta = U_{xyy} - PU_{yyy}. \tag{4.24}$$

The two-argument index of absolute risk aversion is $R^A = -U_{yy}/U_y$. I demonstrate below that *if housing is a normal good, whose demand increases with income under certainty, and preferences exhibit nondecreasing absolute risk aversion with respect to housing ($dR^A/dx \geq 0$), then the covariance is negative so that $\partial x/\partial\sigma < 0$ and income risk reduces housing demand.*

Differentiating the absolute risk-aversion index under the second assumption reveals

$$dR^A/dx = -[U_{yyx} - PU_{yyy}]/U_y + [U_{xy} - PU_{yy}]U_{yy}/U_y^2 \geq 0. \tag{4.25}$$

The normality assumption implies $[U_{xy} - PU_{yy}] > 0$, whereas risk aversion requires $U_{yy} < 0$; thus, the entire second term in (4.25) is negative. Therefore, for (4.25) to hold, the entire first term must be positive. Because $U_y > 0$, the first term will be positive if the RHS of (4.24) is negative. But this in turn requires that $\partial x/\partial\sigma < 0$, as asserted.

---

### 4.4 CONSUMER CHOICE UNDER PRICE UNCERTAINTY

I now turn to the uncertain housing price case. Assume income is certain, but the user cost of housing may vary quicker than adjustments can be made in housing consumption (that is, the level of housing consumption incurred as an obligation). Housing price is $P + \theta$, where $P$ is nonstochastic and $\theta$ is the stochastic term distributed with zero mean and variance $VAR(\theta)$. Housing consumption is again set ex ante. The ex post budget constraint is $I = (P + \theta)x + y$, so that $y = I - (P + \theta)x$ and nonhousing consumption is the risky good, with mean $E[y] = I - Px$ and variance $VAR(y) = x^2 VAR(\theta)$. Thus, unlike the income risk case just considered, the housing price risk case introduces multiplicative risk; the consumer's total risk exposure rises with housing consumption ($dVAR(y)/dx = 2xVAR(\theta) > 0$), leading to a marginal risk cost of additional housing consumption above the usual expected rental price. This simple change to the model complicates the analysis considerably.

Solving the ex post budget constraint for $y = I - (P + \theta)x$ and substituting into the expected utility function, the consumer's problem is

$$\max_x E\{U[x, I - (P + \theta)x]\}. \tag{4.26}$$

The solution to this problem is the Marshallian housing demand, which is a function of expected price, income, and the level of price risk, or $x(P, I, \sigma)$. This demand function satisfies the FOC for problem (4.26), which is

$$E[U_x] - E[(P + \theta)U_y] = 0. \tag{4.27}$$

As in the income uncertainty model, *planned* nonhousing consumption can be defined as $m = E[y] = I - Px$. Using this notation, the Hicksian demands are defined by

$$\{X(P, E[U], \sigma), M(P, E[U], \sigma)\} \equiv \text{argmin } Px + m \text{ s.t. } E[U]$$
$$= E[U(x, m + \theta x)]. \tag{4.28}$$

Following the procedure used for the income uncertainty model step-by-step, the housing demand properties needed for further analysis in chapter 5 can be shown as, specifically:

1. *Demand duality.* For $E[U^*]$, the maximum expected utility from (4.26):

$$x(P, \Omega(P, E[U^*], \sigma), \sigma) \equiv X(P, E[U^*], \sigma).$$

2. *Substitution Theorem.* The effect of expected housing price on Hicksian housing demand is negative under price uncertainty: $\partial X/\partial P < 0$.
3. *Slutsky equation.* The effect of expected housing price on Marshallian housing demand satisfies the Slutsky equation under price uncertainty:

$$\partial x/\partial P = \partial X/\partial P - x(\partial x/\partial I).$$

To find the effect of a mean preserving increase in the housing price distribution spread, substitute $\sigma\theta$ for $\theta$ in (4.27), then differentiate and evaluate the result at $\sigma = 1$. The result is:

$$\partial x/\partial \sigma = E\{[U_{xy} - U_{yy}(P + \theta)]\theta x\}/D + E[U_y\theta]/D, \tag{4.29}$$

with $D = E[U_{xx}] - 2E[U_{xy}(P + \theta)] + E[U_{yy}(P + \theta)^2] < 0$. The first term in (4.29) represents the risk income effect; the second term represents the risk substitution effect.

Intuitively, the risk substitution effect arises here because the risky housing price implies risky nonhousing consumption, recalling the variance of which is $VAR(y) = x^2VAR(\theta)$. Clearly, greater housing consumption penalizes the consumer by increasing the riskiness of nonhousing consumption [i.e., $dVAR(y)/dx = 2xVAR(\sigma\theta) > 0$], providing the marginal risk cost of housing. Recognizing this, greater housing risk in the form of greater variance $VAR(\sigma\theta)$ is also seen to increase the marginal risk cost of housing, the marginal effect of which induces the consumer to substitute away from housing even when the level of total risk is held unchanged. This risk substitution effect, the second term in (4.29), is unambiguously negative in general.

Now consider the risk income effect. Recall that the risk income effect arises because greater price risk increases the *level* of nonhousing consumption risk that the consumer must endure at each possible housing consumption rate. The consumer's response to the greater risk level, holding the marginal risk cost of x unchanged, is the risk income effect, captured by the first term in (4.29). This term is identical in construction to the additive income risk effect in the preceding model of income uncertainty (see [4.23]), except for the addition of the stochastic term in the gross housing price here. This similarity, of course, is the reason for identifying the first term in (4.29) as a type of risk income effect.

What appears from this relationship is that just as goods may be considered "normal" or "inferior" in response to changes in money income, they may be considered normal or inferior in the risk income effect sense. The logical extension of this analysis is to turn to the conditions associated with risk normality (or inferiority), with an eye toward sufficient conditions to arrive at a determinate risk effect (4.29). Turnbull et al. (1991) showed that $\partial x/\partial\sigma < 0$ under the assumptions that housing is a normal good and nondecreasing partial relative risk aversion with respect to housing.

## 4.5 CONSUMER CHOICE UNDER CONSUMPTION RISK

Consider now the effect of consumption risk in housing. The quantity of housing capital purchased by the consumer is z. The actual or ex post housing service generated by a unit of housing capital purchased is $\theta$, which is uncertain at the time housing purchase (or rent) plans are made. Because θ is per unit of z, ex post housing consumption, x, is simply

$$x = \theta z. \tag{4.30}$$

The stochastic term is positive, with $E[\theta] = 1$ and variance $VAR(\theta)$. In this model of housing consumption risk, the expected value of housing consumption is the level of planned consumption, $E[x] = E[\theta]z = z$, and the variance is $VAR(x) = VAR(\theta z) = z^2 VAR(\theta)$. Thus, increases in planned consumption increase the expected level of consumption as well as the variance of consumption.

Assuming income and housing price are known with certainty, the consumer's problem is to select z and y to maximize expected utility $E[U(x, y)]$ subject to the budget constraint, $I = Pz + y$ and (4.30). Solving the budget constraint for y and substituting with (4.30) into the expected utility function, the consumer's problem can be written

$$\max_z E[U(\theta z, I - Pz)]. \tag{4.31}$$

The optimal planned housing consumption is a function of housing price, income, and consumption risk (indexed by σ), or $z(P, I, \sigma)$. Planned housing demand therefore satisfies the FOC obtained by differentiating (4.31) with respect to z:

$$E[U_x \theta] - PE[U_y] = 0. \tag{4.32}$$

Using $y(P, I, \sigma) = I - Pz(P, I, \sigma)$, the optimal expected utility level is

$$E[U^*] = E\{U[\theta z(P, I, \sigma), y(P, I, \sigma)]\}. \tag{4.33}$$

### Demand Duality under Consumption Risk

I define the Hicksian planned housing and nonhousing demands, Z and Y:

$$[Z(P, E[U]; \sigma), Y(P, E[U]; \sigma)] \equiv \text{argmin } Pz + y \text{ s.t. } E[U]$$
$$= EU(x, y); x = \theta z. \tag{4.34}$$

These demands are the unique implicit solutions to the FOC:

$$P - \lambda E[U_x \theta] = 0, \tag{4.35}$$

$$1 - \lambda E[U_y] = 0, \text{ and} \tag{4.36}$$

$$E[U] - EU(\theta z, y) = 0, \tag{4.37}$$

where $\lambda$ is the Lagrangian multiplier. Substituting the solutions to these conditions into the objective function yields the expenditure function

$$e(P, E[U], \sigma) = PZ(P, E[U], \sigma) + Y(P, E[U], \sigma). \quad (4.38)$$

The following results can be proved using the general procedures followed for the income uncertainty model (Turnbull 1991).

1. *Demand duality.* For $E[U^*]$, the maximum expected utility (4.33):

$$z(P, e(P, E[U^*], \sigma), \sigma) \equiv Z(P, E[U^*], \sigma). \quad (4.39)$$

2. *Substitution Theorem.* The Hicksian or pure substitution effect of housing price on planned housing consumption is negative: $(\partial Z/\partial P) < 0$.
3. *Slutsky equation.* The Slutsky equation for planned housing demand (4.70) under quality uncertainty is

$$(\partial z/\partial P) = (\partial Z/\partial P) - z(\partial z/\partial I^o). \quad (4.40)$$

**Consumption Risk Effect on Housing Demand**

The standard approach is used to find the effect of an increase in quality uncertainty on housing demand. Substitute $\theta = (1 + \sigma\epsilon)$ into the model, where $\epsilon$ is now the stochastic term with $E[\epsilon] = 0$ and variance $VAR(\epsilon)$. Note that $VAR(\theta) = \sigma^2 VAR(\epsilon)$. Treating $\sigma$ as a shift parameter, increases in $\sigma$ evaluated at $\sigma = 1$ increase the variance of housing consumption outcomes while leaving the mean consumption level unchanged ($d VAR(x)/d\sigma = VAR(\epsilon) > 0$ and $dE[x]/d\sigma = 0$). Implicit differentiation of (4.32) evaluated at $\sigma = 1$ yields

$$dz/d\sigma = -E[U_x(\theta - 1)]/D - zE[((U_{xx}\theta - PU_{yx})(\theta - 1)]/D, \quad (4.41)$$

where $D = E[U_{xx}\theta^2] + P^2E[U_{yy}] - 2PE[U_{xy}\theta] < 0$ under the concavity assumption. Recall that $E[\theta] = 1$, as before. The first term is the risk substitution effect, while the second is the risk income effect.

The risk substitution effect arises because greater riskiness in housing consumption increases the relative riskiness of housing vis-à-vis nonhousing consumption; hence, the expected marginal rate of substitution between housing and nonhousing consumption, prodding the household to substitute away from housing even when compensated to remain at an unchanged level of total riskiness. Because $E[U_x(\theta - 1)] = E[U_x]E[\theta - 1] + COV[U_x, \theta - 1]$, the fact that $E[\theta - 1] = 0$ further implies that the first term in (4.41) takes the sign of the covariance. Using the properties of similar/dissimilar orderings, though, the covariance takes the sign of $U_{xx}$, so that under risk aversion (i.e., $U_{xx} < 0$), the risk substitution effect is negative.

The risk income effect arises from the greater level of riskiness in housing consumption at all planned consumption levels. We are interested in the conditions sufficient to establish a negative risk income effect reinforcing the negative substitution effect. Using $E[\theta] = 1$, the second term in (4.41) clearly takes the sign as $COV[U_{xx}\theta - PU_{yx}, \theta - 1]$. Drawing from the properties of similar/dissimilar orderings, the sign of the covariance term is

$$\begin{aligned} \text{sgn [COV]} &= \text{sgn } [\partial(U_{xx}\theta - PU_{yx})/\partial\theta] \\ &= \text{sgn } [U_{xx} + z(U_{xxx}\theta - PU_{yxx})]. \end{aligned} \quad (4.42)$$

The index of relative risk aversion for the two-argument utility function is $R^R = -\theta z U_{xx}/U_x$. The value of this index changes with planned consumption as

$$\begin{aligned} dR^R/dz = &-[\theta U_{xx} + \theta z(U_{xxx}\theta - PU_{yxx})]/U_x \\ &- \theta z U_{xx}[U_{xx}\theta - PU_{yx}]/U_x^2. \quad (4.43) \end{aligned}$$

Using the traditional consumer model, the entire second term (with minus sign) is negative if housing is a normal good in the certainty model. Thus, nondecreasing relative risk aversion with respect to planned housing consumption, or $dR^R/dz \geq 0$, is sufficient for the first term in (4.43) to be positive. But this implies that the final expression in (4.42) is negative; (4.42) would therefore be negative and the second term in (4.41), the risk income effect, would be negative as well. In sum, $(\partial z/\partial\sigma) < 0$: *Again it is shown that the noninferiority of housing in the risk income effect sense is sufficient to establish a negative relationship between risk and quantity demanded, and that this "risk income effect" noninferiority notion rests with the characterization of constant or increasing relative risk aversion with respect to planned housing consumption in conjunction with housing being a normal good in the traditional sense.*

---

### 4.6 CONCLUDING REMARKS

This chapter has provided a complete introduction to the expected utility model of uncertainty. Sections 4.1 and 4.2 explained the single-variable expected utility paradigm and its immediate application for housing demand analysis. Given the foundation presented in the first two sections, sections 4.3–4.5 focused primarily on the multiple-argument expected utility function. Following presentation of the general method, specific results needed for subsequent spatial analysis in chapter 5 were derived and explained.

This chapter contributes to methodology as well. The multiple-argument expected utility function model is shown to generate demand functions with economically appealing properties. Expected price, expected income, and the different types of uncertainties generate comparative static effects that are shown to depend upon the properties of demand under certainty. Exploiting the relationship between certainty and uncertainty models, the discussion illustrates how the analysis of behavior under uncertainty may gain wider acceptance and usage than is likely when relying solely upon purely mathematical or technical conditions whose economic content is otherwise often elusive.

---

### Notes

1. An interior solution requires $E[\theta] > r$. If the expected return on the risky asset is less than or equal to the return on the certain asset, any risk-averse consumer will always put all of his or her wealth into the certain asset.

2. CARA or DARA requires $dR^A/d\omega = [U''(\omega)/U'(\omega)]^2 - U'''(\omega)/U'(\omega) \leq 0$, which in turn requires that $U''' > 0$.

# Chapter Five

# LOCATION CHOICE UNDER UNCERTAINTY

This chapter presents the theory of location demand under uncertainty. As pointed out in chapter 4, the introduction of uncertainty into the urban residential location paradigm is necessary because of the nature of housing consumption. Housing represents a durable consumer good, comprising capital and land inputs. The key characteristic is that, because housing is so durable, urban consumers cannot readily adjust housing and residential location decisions to short-term variations in income, in the user cost of housing, in housing quality, in neighborhood externalities, or in household tastes. Recognizing that households do not know all of these factors with certainty when making housing consumption and location decisions, a handful of analyses, most of them recent, have formally investigated uncertainty effects on housing and location demands. As the motivating factors underlying the uncertainty vary, so have the types of uncertainty envisioned in each study. Using a unified theoretical structure, this chapter integrates the major areas studied in the theoretical literature: income uncertainty (Andrulis 1982; DeSalvo and Eeckhoudt 1982; Turnbull et al. 1991), housing user cost uncertainty (Turnbull et al. 1991), transportation cost uncertainty (Papageorgiou and Pines 1988), and uncertain quality and neighborhood externalities (Papageorgiou 1991; Turnbull 1991).

---

## 5.1 INCOME UNCERTAINTY

Several attempts have been made to model housing demand with uncertain income. Andrulis (1982) focused on the household's incentive to relocate within the urban area, moving from a previously optimal housing and location combination in response to new information or a changed state of nature. By concentrating on the decision to move per se, Andrulis concluded that, because risk aversion enters

the model via second-order derivatives and since the location equilibrium condition involves only first-order derivatives, risk attitude
(hence, presumably, the level of uncertainty itself) "plays no role in
characterizing location equilibrium" (p. 90). As demonstrated here,
his conclusion is erroneous; both risk and risk attitude play fundamental roles in housing and location demand behavior.

In the first complete theoretical analysis of income uncertainty in
the urban location context, DeSalvo and Eeckhoudt (1982) analyzed
the effect of unemployment risk on housing and location demand.
Turnbull et al. (1991) extended that work in several directions. First,
DeSalvo and Eeckhoudt allowed only for two possible income states,
high or low, reflecting "employed" or "unemployed" states or outcomes, whereas the latter paper allowed for a variety of possible income outcomes. In addition, the Turnbull et al. income uncertainty
formulation, which is the approach taken here, successfully exploited
the theories outlined in chapters 2 and 4, thereby providing intuitively
meaningful interpretations of the conditions underlying risk effect
comparative statics missing in the earlier work.

## Model of Income Uncertainty

I return to the certainty model detailed in chapter 2, retaining that
notation with the exception that household income is assumed to be
uncertain at the time that housing consumption and location decisions are made. Household income is $I + \theta$, where $I$ is known with
certainty while $\theta$ is stochastic, with zero mean and finite variance
($E[\theta] = 0$, $VAR(\theta) > 0$). Household income is therefore uncertain, ex
ante, with mean $E[I + \theta] = I$ and variance $VAR(I + \theta) = VAR(\theta)$.

Once $\theta$ is realized, the household consumes the chosen housing $x^*$
at location $k^*$ and nonhousing goods $y$ such that the budget constraint
is fulfilled ex post. More formally, the household's problem is

$$\max_{x,k} EU(x, y) \quad \text{s.t.} \quad I + \theta = P(k)x + y + T(k), \qquad (5.1)$$

where the expectation is taken over $\theta$. The effect of binding survival
and/or bankruptcy constraints on consumer behavior is examined
later in the chapter.

Following the procedure in chapter 2, break problem (5.1) into a
two-stage problem by defining

$$x(P, I^0; \sigma) = \text{argmax } EU[x, I - T(k) - P(k)x + \theta], \qquad (5.2)$$

where $I^0 = E[I - T(k) + \theta]$ is the expected net of transportation cost
household income and $\sigma$ is a parameter describing the riskiness em-

bodied in $\theta$ (that is, the variance of the $\theta$ distribution). The indirect expected utility is found by substituting (5.2) into the original expected utility function to obtain

$$\Phi[P(k), I - T(k)] = EU[x(P, I^0;\sigma), I^0 - P(k)x(P, I^0;\sigma) + \theta]. \quad (5.3)$$

The household's optimal location maximizes (5.3), and is the solution to

$$d\Phi/dk = E[U_y(-P_k x - T_k)] = 0. \quad (5.4)$$

The location demand is implicitly a function of the income risk parameter: $k^* = k(\sigma)$. Substituting into (5.2) yields the housing demand, which completes the solution to problem (5.1):

$$x^* = x[P(k^*), I^0(k^*);\sigma]. \quad (5.5)$$

**Housing Demand Gradient and Housing Price Function**

The optimal location satisfies (5.4), which reduces to Muth's equation:

$$-P_k x - T_k = 0. \quad (5.6)$$

As in the certainty case, $T_k > 0$ requires $P_k < 0$, so that *housing price declines with distance from the central business district (CBD)*. The introduction of additive income risk does not alter this important qualitative conclusion of the certainty model.

The housing demand gradient is evaluated by differentiating demand (5.2) with respect to distance, yielding

$$\partial x/\partial k = (\partial x/\partial P)P_k - (\partial x/\partial I^0)T_k \quad (5.7)$$

Solving (5.6) for $T_k$ and substituting into (5.7):

$$\partial x/\partial k = [(\partial x/\partial P) + x(\partial x/\partial I^0)]P_k. \quad (5.8)$$

Section 4.3 showed that the Slutsky equation holds for housing demand (5.2) under income uncertainty:

$$\partial x/\partial P = (\partial X/\partial P) - x(\partial x/\partial I^0), \quad (5.9)$$

where $X$ is the compensated housing demand (holding location unchanged) and $\partial X/\partial P < 0$ is the compensated own-price effect under uncertainty. Rearranging (5.9) and substituting for the bracketed expression in (5.8) yields:

$$\partial x/\partial k = (\partial X/\partial P)P_k > 0, \quad (5.10)$$

and housing demand increases with distance, as in the certainty model.

Turning to the curvature properties of the housing price function under uncertainty, the second-order condition (SOC) for the optimal location is $d^2\Phi/dk^2 = \Phi_{kk} < 0$, which requires:

$$-P_{kk}x - P_k(\partial x/\partial k) - T_{kk} < 0. \tag{5.11}$$

But $T_{kk} \leq 0$, while $P_k < 0$ and $\partial x/\partial k > 0$ are shown above. Therefore, for (5.11) to hold, it must be true that $P_{kk} > 0$: *the housing price function under income uncertainty is convex with respect to distance,* a prediction consistent with the certainty case.

**Income Risk Effects**

To find the effect of a pure increase in income risk on consumer demand for housing and location, consider the mean preserving spread explained in the "Income Risk Effects" subsection of section 4.3. Replace the stochastic term $\theta$ with $\sigma\theta$, where $\sigma$ is a nonstochastic parameter. The variance of the new term $\sigma\theta$ is therefore $\sigma^2\text{VAR}(\theta)$, and increases in $\sigma$ yield increases in the spread of the distribution of the stochastic term without altering the expected net income:

$$dE[I - T(k) + \sigma\theta]/d\sigma = dE[I - T(k)]/d\sigma = 0$$

$$d\text{VAR}(\sigma\theta)/d\sigma = 2\sigma\text{VAR}(\theta) > 0.$$

To find the effect of an increase in income uncertainty or risk, consider $d\sigma > 0$ evaluated at $\sigma = 1$.

Substituting (5.2) into Muth's equation (5.6), then differentiating, reveals the effect of greater income risk on location demand:

$$dk^*/d\sigma = -P_k(\partial x/\partial\sigma)/[P_{kk}x + P_k(\partial x/\partial k) + T_{kk}]. \tag{5.12}$$

Differentiating spatial housing demand with endogenous location (5.5) yields the total effect of income risk on housing demand:

$$dx^*/d\sigma = (\partial x/\partial\sigma) + (\partial x/\partial k)(dk^*/d\sigma)$$

$$= (\partial x/\partial\sigma) - P_k^2(\partial X/\partial P)(\partial x/\partial\sigma)/[P_{kk}x \tag{5.13}$$

$$+ P_k(\partial x/\partial k) + T_{kk}],$$

where the second line follows by substituting (5.10) and (5.12). Two points are evident: first, the indirect effect of income risk on housing demand through location choice (the second term in [5.13]) reinforces the direct effect (first term); and, second, risk effects on location (5.12) and housing demand (5.13) are determined by the direct effect of the risk effect on Marshallian demand, $\partial x/\partial \sigma$. As demonstrated in the "Income Risk Effects" subsection of section 4.3, risk normality ensures $\partial x/\partial \sigma < 0$, leading to the conclusion that $dk^*/d\sigma < 0$ and $dx^*/d\sigma < 0$. Greater income risk increases demand for central business district (CBD) proximimity and decreases housing demand.

Greater income risk lowers housing demand at each distance, shifting the consumption gradient downward from $x(k)$ to $x(k)'$ in the left-hand panel of figure 5.1. The lower housing demand at each $k$, in turns, lowers the marginal benefit of distance (MBD), in the right panel. The lower MBD prods the household to live closer to the CBD, from $k_1$ to $k_3$. By itself, the move closer to the CBD increases housing price, which lowers housing demand so that this indirect effect of income risk on housing demand from $x^2$ to $x^3$ reinforces the direct effect, the change from $x^1$ to $x^2$ due to the risk-induced shift in the consumption gradient. As can be seen from the figure, the indirect or location effect of risky income always reinforces the direct effect.

Some empirical evidence is relevant here. Haurin and Gill (1987) used data on military families to examine how expected income and income uncertainty affect housing demand. They considered two-income families, assuming income of military service personnel is less uncertain than the nonmilitary secondary worker's income. Their finding that expected military salary yields a greater marginal propensity to consume housing than expected nonmilitary secondary

Figure 5.1 INCOME UNCERTAINTY EFFECTS ON HOUSING AND LOCATION

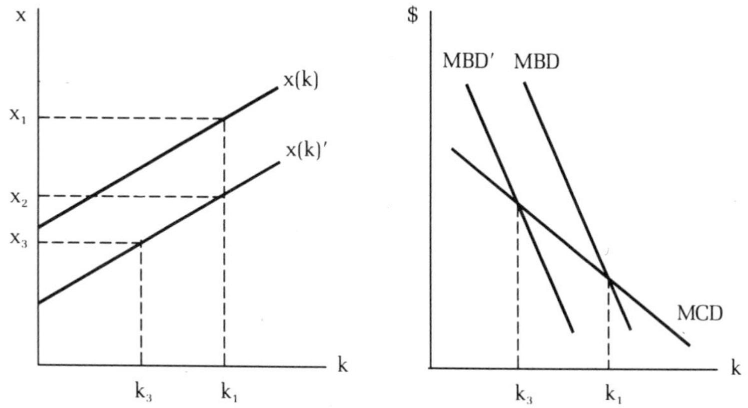

Notes: MDB, marginal benefit of distance; MCD, marginal cost of distance.

income reveals that income uncertainty does reduce housing demand. This is predicted by this study's model.

## Other Comparative Statics

The comparative static results of Turnbull et al. (1991) generalized those of DeSalvo and Eeckhoudt (1982), who considered only the dichotomous income case (that is, "employed" and "unemployed" as the only possible states). As in the certainty theory of chapter 2, introduce a shift parameter $\alpha$ to capture changes in housing price, transportation costs, tastes, and expected income. The location change induced by a change in $\alpha$ is found in the normal manner, by implicitly differentiating Muth's equation to find $dk^*/d\alpha$. The housing demand change then follows by differentiating (5.5), recalling that $k^*$ is itself endogenous and will change as $\alpha$ changes in the analysis. From (5.5) one obtains

$$dx^*/d\alpha = (\partial x/\partial \alpha) + P_k(\partial X/\partial P)(dk^*/d\alpha), \qquad (5.14)$$

and the total effect of $\alpha$ on housing demand comprises the direct effect $\partial x/\partial \alpha$, holding location unchanged, and the indirect or location effect, which is the second term in (5.14). The comparative static results are summarized in table 5.1.

### HOUSING PRICE CHANGES

Specify $P(k, \alpha)$ with $\partial P/\partial \alpha = P_\alpha > 0$ depicting an increase in housing price at all distances. Differentiating Muth's equation yields

Table 5.1  COMPARATIVE STATIC EFFECTS UNDER UNCERTAINTY

| Increase in: | Sufficient Conditions | Housing $x^*$ | Location |
|---|---|---|---|
| Housing price | $P_{k\alpha} \geq 0$ | — | — |
| | $P_{k\alpha} < 0$ | ? | ? |
| Income | | + | + |
| Commuting costs | $T_{k\alpha} \geq 0$ | — | — |
| | $T_{k\alpha} < 0$ | ? | ? |
| Housing tastes | | + | + |
| Income risk | Marshallian risk normality | — | — |
| Price risk | Marshallian risk normality | — | — |
|   Increasing with distance | | — | — |
|   Decreasing with distance | | + | + |
| Travel cost risk | Marshallian risk normality | — | — |
|   Increasing with distance | | — | — |
|   Decreasing with distance | | + | + |
| Housing quality risk | Marshallian risk normality | — | — |

$$dk^*/d\alpha = [P_{k\alpha}x(P, I^0) + P_k P_\alpha(\partial x/\partial P)]/\Phi_{kk}E[U_y]^{-1}, \qquad (5.15)$$

with $\phi_{kk} < 0$ and $E[U_y] > 0$, while (5.14) becomes

$$dx^*/d\alpha = (\partial x/\partial P)P_\alpha + P_k(\partial X/\partial P)(dk^*/d\alpha). \qquad (5.16)$$

As in the certainty case, if a rise in $\alpha$ does not make the price gradient steeper ($P_{k\alpha} \geq 0$), then $dk^*/d\alpha < 0$ and $dx^*/d\alpha < 0$, assuming housing is not a Giffen good in the consumer choice model without location choice. The intuition here follows that for the certainty case investigated in chapter 2.

### TRANSPORTATION COST CHANGES

Specify transportation costs by $T(k, \alpha)$ with shift parameter $\alpha$ and $T_\alpha > 0$. Following the same procedure as above, differentiate Muth's equation for location equilibrium to find the effect of transportation cost increases on location demand

$$dk^*/d\alpha = [P_k(\partial x/\partial I^0)(dI^0/d\alpha) + T_{k\alpha}]/\Phi_{kk}E[U_y]^{-1}. \qquad (5.17)$$

But $I^0 = I - T(k, \alpha)$ by definition, $dI^0/d\alpha = -T_\alpha$, and (5.17) becomes

$$dk^*/d\alpha = [-P_k(\partial x/\partial I^0)T_\alpha + T_{k\alpha}]/\Phi_{kk}E[U_y]^{-1}. \qquad (5.18)$$

Recall that $\Phi_{kk} < 0$ and $E[U_y] > 0$. Thus, a shift in the transportation cost function that does not decrease the marginal cost of distance, $T_{k\alpha} \geq 0$, is sufficient to establish $dk^*/d\alpha < 0$. The intuition here is as follows. An increase in travel cost lowers net income, which by itself tends to decrease housing demand at each distance, thereby decreasing the MBD; an increase in the marginal cost of distance reinforces the effect of lower MBD on optimal distance, and $k^*$ declines as a result. Equation (5.14) reveals that the location effect reinforces the direct effect of lower net income on housing demand, and $T_{k\alpha} \geq 0$ is sufficient to establish $dx^*/d\alpha < 0$ as well.

### TASTE CHANGES

Introduce the shift parameter into $x(P, I^0, \alpha)$ so that $\partial x/\partial \alpha > 0$ indicates stronger tastes for housing. The effect of stronger tastes for housing on location and housing demand are therefore:

$$dk^*/d\alpha = P_k(\partial x/\partial \alpha)/\Phi_{kk}E[U_y]^{-1} > 0 \qquad (5.19)$$

$$dx^*/d\alpha = (\partial x/\partial \alpha) + P_k^2(\partial X/\partial P)(\partial x/\partial \alpha)/\Phi_{kk}E[U_y]^{-1} > 0. \qquad (5.20)$$

The location effect of stronger housing tastes reinforces the direct effect so that the household consumes a greater amount of housing services farther out from the CBD.

### EXPECTED INCOME CHANGES

Recall that $T_{kI} = 0$ in the uncertainty model here. The income effects on location and housing demands are therefore

$$dk^*/d\alpha = P_k(\partial x/\partial I^o)/\Phi_{kk}E[U_y]^{-1} > 0 \tag{5.21}$$

$$dx^*/d\alpha = (\partial x/\partial I^o) + P_k^2(\partial X/\partial P)(\partial x/\partial I^o)/\Phi_{kk}E[U_y]^{-1} > 0. \tag{5.22}$$

The household resides farther away from the CBD and consumes a greater quantity of housing at the higher income. These results are identical to the certainty model income comparative statics for $T_{kI} = 0$.

---

### 5.2 HOUSING PRICE UNCERTAINTY

I now turn to the effect of uncertain housing price on location choice and housing demand. As pointed out in the previous chapter, Henderson and Ioannides (1983) provided a nonspatial analysis of housing demand under rate-of-return uncertainty. Their model explicitly combines both the consumption and investment motives for acquiring housing. The consumption motive for acquiring housing is modeled in the usual fashion, that is, as the selection of x and y maximizing consumption utility $U(x, y)$. Because housing services are garnered from the durable housing asset whose market value may rise or fall over the consumption period, net future wealth is also affected by the choice of housing stock. This investment motive for acquiring housing is captured in the Henderson-Ioannides model by appending the portfolio investment model related to the expected utility function $E[\phi(\omega)]$ in section 4.2, where $\omega$ is future wealth, which is uncertain because of the uncertain return to investment in housing. A composite utility function, $U(x, y) + E[\phi(\omega)]$, captures both consumption and investment motives and serves as the objective function for the consumer-investor's behavior. Although their focus is tenure choice, the general approach is in the spirit of the price risk model of Turnbull et al. (1991), explained in this section. Unlike the Henderson and Ioannides model, the analysis here is explicitly spatial.

To begin the analysis of consumer behavior under housing price uncertainty, note that as in the uncertain income case, the household makes housing and location choices ex ante and cannot revise these obligations after the stochastic term $\theta$ is realized. The stochastic term as used in this section reflects uncertainty over unavoidable maintenance and repairs, property taxes, fees, and unavoidable utilities over the consumption period. It also reflects uncertainty over the user price of housing induced by stochastic capital gains or losses on housing assets; therefore, this model does capture the investment motive for acquiring housing stock in addition to the consumption motive.

## Model of Housing Price Uncertainty

This section considers the case where price uncertainty does not vary with distance. Housing price is simply $P(k) + \theta$, where $P(k)$ is nonstochastic, and $\theta$ is the stochastic term with zero mean and finite variance (i.e., $E[\theta] = 0$ and $VAR(\theta) \geq 0$, as before). Expected housing price is $E[P(k) + \theta] = P(k)$, whereas the variance of housing price is $VAR[P(k) + \theta] = VAR(\theta)$, which is spatially invariant, $dVAR[P + \theta]/dk = 0$.

As in previous discussions in this volume, I defer consideration of binding survival constraints until later in the chapter. Given an interior solution, then, housing demand at any given location is defined by

$$x(P, I^0;\sigma) \equiv argmax \, EU(x, I - T(k) - [P(k) + \theta]x). \quad (5.23)$$

Substituting into the expected utility function to obtain the indirect expected utility function

$$\Phi[P(k), I - T(k)]$$

$$= EU(x(P, I^0;\sigma), I - T(k) - [P(k) + \theta]x(P, I^0;\sigma)) \quad (5.24)$$

the household's optimal location satisfies the first-order condition (FOC)

$$\Phi_k = E[U_y(-P_k x - T_k)] = 0. \quad (5.25)$$

The optimal housing consumption is found by substituting $k^*$ from (5.25) into (5.23):

$$x^* = x[P(k^*), I^0(k^*);\sigma]. \quad (5.26)$$

## Housing Demand Gradient and Housing Price Function

The optimal location condition simplifies to the familiar certainty version of Muth's equation. Thus, general spatial characteristics of housing price can be derived as a consequence of location equilibrium using the same method as for the income uncertainty model. Differentiating (5.23) with respect to distance yields

$$\partial x/\partial k = (\partial x/\partial P)P_k - (\partial x/\partial I^0)T_k. \tag{5.27}$$

Substituting $T_k = -P_k x$ from the location equilibrium condition into (5.27) reveals

$$\partial x/\partial k = [(\partial x/\partial P) + x(\partial x/\partial I^0)]P_k. \tag{5.28}$$

Because the Slutsky equation holds for the nonspatial consumer choice model under price uncertainty (section 4.4), the term in square brackets equals $(\partial X/\partial P)$, and (5.28) can be rewritten as

$$\partial x/\partial k = (\partial X/\partial P)P_k > 0 \tag{5.29}$$

where the sign of (5.29) follows from the Substitution Theorem (see chapter 4) and $P_k < 0$. This result resembles analogous spatial patterns of housing demand in the certainty and uncertain income models: *under housing price uncertainty the housing demand increases with distance from the CBD.*

Turning to the spatial characteristics of the expected housing price surface,

$$P_k = -T_k/x < 0,$$

from Muth's equation, while

$$P_{kk} = -T_{kk}/x + (\partial x/\partial k)T_k/x^2 > 0,$$

using $T_{kk} \leq 0$ and (5.29). Thus, as in previous cases, *expected price is found to decline and is convex in distance;* the housing price predictions of the certainty model remain surprisingly robust with respect to both income and price uncertainty.

**Price Risk Effects**

To find the price risk effect on housing and location demand, replace $\theta$ with $\sigma\theta$, so that $d\sigma > 0$ yields a mean preserving spread. Differentiate (5.25) and (5.26) to find:

$$dk^*/d\sigma = -P_k(\partial x/\partial \sigma)/[P_{kk}x + P_k(\partial x/\partial k) + T_{kk}] \tag{5.30}$$

$$dx^*/d\sigma = (\partial x/\partial \sigma) - P_k^2(\partial X/\partial P)(\partial x/\partial \sigma)/[P_{kk}$$
$$+ P_k(\partial x/\partial k) + T_{kk}]. \tag{5.31}$$

As in the risky income case, the indirect effect of price risk via location (the second term in [5.31]) reinforces the direct effect. The effects of price risk on location and housing demand therefore will always be in the same direction, following the sign of the Marshallian risk term $\partial x/\partial \sigma$.

The sign of $\partial x/\partial \sigma$ is evaluated in section 4.4, where risk normality is used to ensure $\partial x/\partial \sigma < 0$. Unlike the income risk case, the total price risk effect on Marshallian housing demand comprises two separate effects: a risk substitution and a risk income effect. Intuitively, the risk substitution effect arises here because the risky housing price implies risky nonhousing consumption, or

$$y = I - T(k) - [P(k) + \sigma\theta]x.$$

The variance of nonhousing consumption is $\text{VAR}(y) = x^2\sigma^2\text{VAR}(\theta)$. Clearly, greater housing consumption penalizes the consumer by increasing the riskiness of nonhousing consumption (i.e., $d\text{VAR}[y]/dx = 2x\sigma^2\text{VAR}[\theta] > 0$), providing the marginal risk cost of housing. Recognizing this, one also notes that greater housing risk in the form of greater variance $\sigma^2\text{VAR}(\theta)$ increases the marginal risk cost of housing, the marginal effect of which induces the consumer to substitute away from housing even when the level of total riskiness is held unchanged. As shown in chapter 4, this risk substitution effect is unambiguously negative.

Now consider the risk income effect in this application. The risk income effect arises because greater price risk, as reflected by a larger variance $\sigma^2\text{VAR}(\theta)$ induced by $d\sigma > 0$, increases the *level* of nonhousing consumption risk that the consumer must endure at each possible housing consumption rate. The consumer's response to the greater risk level, holding the marginal risk cost of $x$ unchanged, is this risk income effect. The complication in the risky price case arises because, just as goods may be considered "normal" or "inferior" in response to changes in money income, they may be considered normal or inferior in the risk income effect sense. The logical extension of this analysis is to turn to the conditions associated with risk normality (or inferiority), with an eye toward sufficient conditions to come up with a determinate risk effect. Turnbull et al. (1991) showed how the assumption that the housing is normal in the usual Marshallian sense, coupled with the assumption that the household exhibits partial relative risk aversion, which is either decreasing or constant in housing consumption, provides sufficient conditions for risk normality.

*This means that price risk alone prods the household to move closer to the CBD. In addition, moving closer to the CBD increases the ex-*

pected housing price, inducing the household to reduce housing demand even more than the direct effect indicates.

## Other Comparative Statics

What is interesting here is that the comparative static predictions for the uncertain housing price model are all qualitatively identical to those of the uncertain income model (see table 5.1). Higher income or more intense taste for housing prompts the household to consume more housing farther away from the CBD. Upward shifts in the expected price or transportation cost functions tend to prod the household to consume less housing and reside closer to the CBD, whereas steeper housing price and transportation cost functions slopes tend to offset these effects and decreases in price and transportation cost functions slopes tend to reinforce them.

---

### 5.3 SPATIAL VARIATION IN HOUSING PRICE RISK

Now consider situations in which housing price risk systematically varies across the urban area. Rachlis and Yezer (1985) found evidence that changes in spatial housing demand patterns over time create spatial patterns in expected price appreciation rates as well; because future spatial housing demand patterns are uncertain ex ante, the riskiness or uncertainty of housing asset price appreciation rates would be expected to also exhibit systematic spatial patterns. Such spatial variation in expected values and variances of asset price appreciation rates represent one source of spatial variation in housing user cost riskiness, or what I label housing price risk.

To include spatial variation in risk in the model, specify housing price as $P(k) + \theta(\delta + \beta k)$, where $\theta$ again represents the stochastic term (with zero mean and finite variance) and $\delta > 0$ and $\beta$ are nonstochastic parameters defining the level and spatial variation in price riskiness, to be explained shortly. The expected housing price remains $E[P + \theta(\delta + \beta k)] = P(k)$ as before. The housing price variance, on the other hand, now becomes $VAR[P + \theta(\delta + \beta k)] = (\delta + \beta k)^2 VAR(\theta)$. Clearly, larger $\delta$ translates into a higher price variance at all locations, whereas $\beta > 0$ indicates increasing housing price risk with distance and $\beta < 0$ indicates decreasing risk with distance. The case in which no spatial variation in risk occurs pertains to $\beta = 0$ (where $\delta = 1$ then pertains to the earlier models).

The Marshallian housing demand is defined as

$$x(P, I^0;\sigma) \tag{5.32}$$
$$\equiv \text{argmax } EU(x, I - T(k) - (P(k) + \theta(\delta + \beta k))x).$$

Substitute (5.32) into the expected utility function to obtain the indirect expected utility function so that the household's optimal location can be shown to satisfy

$$E\{U_y[-P_k x - \theta\beta x - T_k]\} = 0. \tag{5.33}$$

*The location equilibrium condition (5.33) does not reduce to the usual statement of Muth's equation.* Instead, it becomes

$$-P_k x = T_k + \beta x E[U_y \theta]/E[U_y]$$

$$-P_k x = T_k + \beta x \text{COV}[U_y, \theta]/E[U_y],$$

where $E[U_y \theta] = \text{COV}[U_y, \theta] > 0$.[1]

When income or housing price risk are constant across locations, Muth's equation requires that the household locate where the savings from lower housing prices available at greater distance from the CBD just equal the additional commuting cost of moving farther out. When price risk varies with location, though, a third factor (the second RHS term) also weighs in the household's location decision: *the marginal increase or decrease in price risk induced by moving farther away from the CBD.* This change in risk provides an additional cost (benefit) associated with distance for $\beta > 0$ ($\beta < 0$). The location equilibrium condition shows that increasing price risk with distance reinforces the negative slope of expected housing price function, whereas decreasing price risk with distance reduces the expected price slope. In addition, *the expected housing price gradient may be positively inclined at locations where there is a sufficiently steep reduction in price risk with distance* ($\beta < 0$) *and small marginal transportation cost so that* $T_k + \beta x \text{COV}[U_y, \theta]/E[U_y] < 0$. Thus, a flat or increasing expected housing price function may be possible when risk declines with distance from the CBD.

To find the effect of spatial variation in price risk on location and housing demand, use the no-spatial-variation solution $k^*$ as a point of reference. Denoting location $k^*$ as the consumer's choice when $\beta = 0$, I evaluate the household response to introducing spatial risk variation as the comparative statics from a change in $\beta$ (that is, moving to $\beta > 0$ or $\beta < 0$), holding total price risk at $k^*$ unchanged. In so doing, I isolate the effect of spatial variation in price risk alone without concomitant changes in the level of risk at the reference point.

Implicit differentiation of (5.33) evaluated at $\beta = 0$ reveals the change in optimal distance induced by spatial variation in risk as

$$dk^{**}/d\beta = -\{-E[U_{yy}(k^* - k^*)(-P_k x - T_k)]$$
$$- E[U_{xy}P_k(\partial x/\partial\beta)(-P_k x - T_k)] - E[U_y\theta]x \quad (5.34)$$
$$- E[U_y(P_k - \theta\beta)(\partial x/\partial\beta)]\}/\Phi_{kk}.$$

The first term in the numerator is zero. To evaluate the second and fourth terms, note that $(\partial x/\partial\beta) = (\partial x/\partial\sigma)(d\sigma/d\beta)$, where $d\sigma$ again denotes a mean preserving change in housing price risk. But recall that the intent is to measure the effect of a change in spatial variation of risk alone, holding the level of risk unchanged at $k^*$: $d\sigma/d\beta = 0$ by construction so that $\partial x/\partial\beta = 0$ and the second and fourth terms in the numerator reduce to zero. Thus, (5.34) simplifies to

$$dk^{**}/d\beta = E[U_y\theta]x/\Phi_{kk} < 0, \quad (5.35)$$

where the sign follows from COV$[U_y, \theta] > 0$ and $\Phi_{kk} < 0$. *Moving from a situation in which there is no spatial variation in risk to one in which risk increases (decreases) with distance decreases (increases) the household's desired distance from the CBD.*

This result has intuitive appeal. If housing price risk falls with greater distance from the CBD, the lower price risk associated with living farther away from the CBD is an additional marginal benefit of distance, which induces the household to locate closer to the urban periphery. If price risk increases with distance, the increasing risk provides an additional marginal cost of distance above the usual marginal commuting cost. In response, the household locates closer to the CBD. In sum, $\beta < 0$ offsets, whereas $\beta > 0$ reinforces, the effect of price uncertainty alone on location demand.

To derive the effect of spatial variation in risk on housing demand, substitute the optimal location into (5.32) and differentiate to find

$$dx^{**}/d\beta = \partial x/\partial\beta + (\partial x/\partial k)(dk^{**}/d\beta). \quad (5.36)$$

Evaluating at $\delta = 1$ and $\beta = 0$, $\partial x/\partial\beta = 0$ as before, $\partial x/\partial k > 0$ and (5.34) and (5.35) leave $dx^{**}/d\beta < 0$. *Rising price risk with distance reduces housing demand, whereas declining price risk with distance increases housing demand relative to the spatially invariant price risk case.* This result, too, is intuitively appealing.

Graphically, the results for consumer response to decreasing price riskiness with distance are depicted in figure 5.2. The left-hand panel of the figure shows the housing consumption gradient with no spatial

Figure 5.2  EFFECTS OF SPATIAL VARIATION IN PRICE RISK ON HOUSING AND
LOCATION: DECREASING RISK WITH DISTANCE ($\beta < 0$ case)

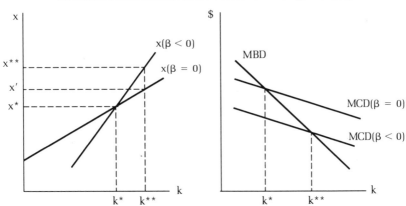

Notes: MDB, marginal benefit of distance; MCD, marginal cost of distance.

risk variation ($\beta = 0$) and the gradient with $\beta < 0$. As depicted, the
latter is steeper than the former, intersecting at $k^*$ (recall that the level
of risk remains unchanged at $[k^*, x^*]$ in the figure). For $k > k^*$ risk
levels along with $\beta < 0$ are less than risk levels along with $\beta = 0$;
$\partial x / \partial \sigma < 0$ leads to greater housing consumption along $\beta = 0$ than
along $\beta < 0$. Similarly, risk is lower along $\beta = 0$ than $\beta < 0$ for $k <$
$k^*$, leading to greater consumption along $\beta = 0$ than $\beta < 0$ for these
locations.

The right-hand panel of figure 5.2 demonstrates that a decrease in
$\beta$ reduces the marginal cost of distance (MCD). (At the same time, but
not shown, $d\beta < 0$ reduces the absolute slope of the MBD curve.) The
lower MCD increases the optimal distance to $k^{**}$. Reading from the
left-hand diagram, the movement from $k^*$ to $k^{**}$ has two discernible
effects on housing demand. First, the lower expected price farther out
stimulates demand from $x^*$ to $x'$. Second, the decrease in risk from
moving farther out also stimulates demand from $x'$ to $x^{**}$, reinforcing
the decreasing expected price effect.

A similar graphical analysis can be presented for the $d\beta > 0$ case.
An increase in $\beta$ shifts the MCD upward, leading to the reduction in
optimal distance, $k^*$ to $k^{**}$ in the right-hand panel. In response to
the higher expected price from locating closer to the CBD, housing
demand falls from $x^*$ to $x'$. However, because the move toward the
CBD reduces risk, housing demand increases from $x'$ to $x^{**}$, offsetting
somewhat the housing demand change induced by the difference in
expected price at the different locations. For both $d\beta > 0$ and $d\beta < 0$

cases, the household location response is to move in the direction of declining price riskiness.

---

## 5.4 QUANTITY CONSTRAINTS

The analysis thus far explicitly assumes that, although many distributions for the stochastic term $\theta$ are allowed, they still satisfy the traditional non-negativity or survival constraints of demand theory. Specifically, if $\theta \in [\theta', \theta'']$, then ex post nonhousing consumption lies on the interval $[y^-, y^+]$, where

$$y^- = I - T(k) + \theta' - P(k)x \qquad (5.37)$$
$$y^+ = I - T(k) + \theta'' - P(k)x.$$

Clearly, $y \geq 0$ for all $\theta$ under the usual non-negativity constraint in order for the model to make economic sense; households cannot consume negative quantities of goods. More generally, nonhousing consumption must attain some minimum non-negative level, say $s$, to ensure survivability (or nonbankruptcy), or $y \geq s$ for all $\theta$. Equivalently, $y^- \geq s$ or

$$I - T(k) + \theta' - Px \geq s, \qquad (5.38)$$

to ensure that the constraint is fulfilled for all realizable $\theta$.

If (5.38) holds with strict inequality at $[x^*, k^*]$, then the constraint is not binding and the earlier analysis pertains. It is not, however, necessary for all previous results to hold when the quantity constraint is binding in equilibrium.

This section investigates the broader implications of quantity constraints for the analysis of location demand under uncertainty. I examine the extent to which such constraints modify established results. The analysis is motivated by a desire to provide a complete partial equilibrium theory of location demand under uncertainty. Nonetheless, the issue of quantity constraints seems particularly relevant to the problem at hand; by selecting sufficiently large housing expenditure obligations, the household may have to face extremely low nonhousing consumption opportunities ex post even when there is a particularly poor (that is, low) realization of $\theta$. It seems reasonable to begin the analysis of how risk-averse households, who recognize the possibility of poor $\theta$ realizations, change their behavior to avoid the penalties associated with the nonsurvivable or bankruptcy outcomes.

## Uncertain Income Case

To begin, consider the situation outlined previously, that of household behavior under income risk. Formally the problem is stated as

$$\max_{x,k} EU(x, y) \quad \text{s.t.} \quad I + \theta = P(k)x + y + T(k); \quad (5.39)$$
$$y \geq 0 \text{ for } \theta \in [\theta', \theta''].$$

Problem (5.39) is a nonlinear programming problem and is equivalent to

$$\max_{x,k} EU(x, I^0 + \theta - Px) \quad \text{s.t.} \quad I^0 + \theta' - Px \geq s, \quad (5.40)$$

where $I^0 + \theta'$ is the lowest possible realized income for the consumer. Following the familiar procedure, the consumption and location choices are considered each in turn.

CONSUMPTION EQUILIBRIUM

The Marshallian housing demand is the solution to the modified problem:

$$\max_x EU(x, I^0 + \theta - Px) \quad \text{s.t.} \quad I^0 + \theta' - Px \geq s. \quad (5.41)$$

The appropriate Lagrangian function for this problem is

$$L(x, \lambda) = EU(x, I^0 + \theta - Px) + \lambda[I^0 + \theta' - Px - s], \quad (5.42)$$

where $\lambda$ is the Kuhn-Tucker multiplier. Given the strict concavity of the utility function in $x$, the following Kuhn-Tucker conditions are both necessary and sufficient for optimality:

$$\partial L/\partial x = E[U_x] - PE[U_y] - \lambda P = 0 \text{ and} \quad (5.43)$$
$$\partial L/\partial \lambda = I^0 + \theta' - Px - s \geq 0;$$

$$(\partial L/\partial \lambda)\lambda = 0; \quad \text{and } \lambda \geq 0. \quad (5.44)$$

The first condition yields, upon rearrangement,

$$E[U_x]/E[U_y] = P + \lambda P/E[U_y]. \quad (5.45)$$

The left-hand-side term is the marginal rate of substitution $(MRS)_{x,y}$ as measured at a point on the expected utility indifference curves in figure 5.3. Notice that the expected utility map is presented in $x - E[y]$ space, as distinguished from the usual characterization in $x - y$ space.

What is of central interest here is the situation in which the quantity constraint is binding, as in figure 5.3. Suppose $s > E[y'] + \theta'$, as

Figure 5.3  CONSUMPTION EQUILIBRIUM UNDER BINDING QUANTITY
CONSTRAINT

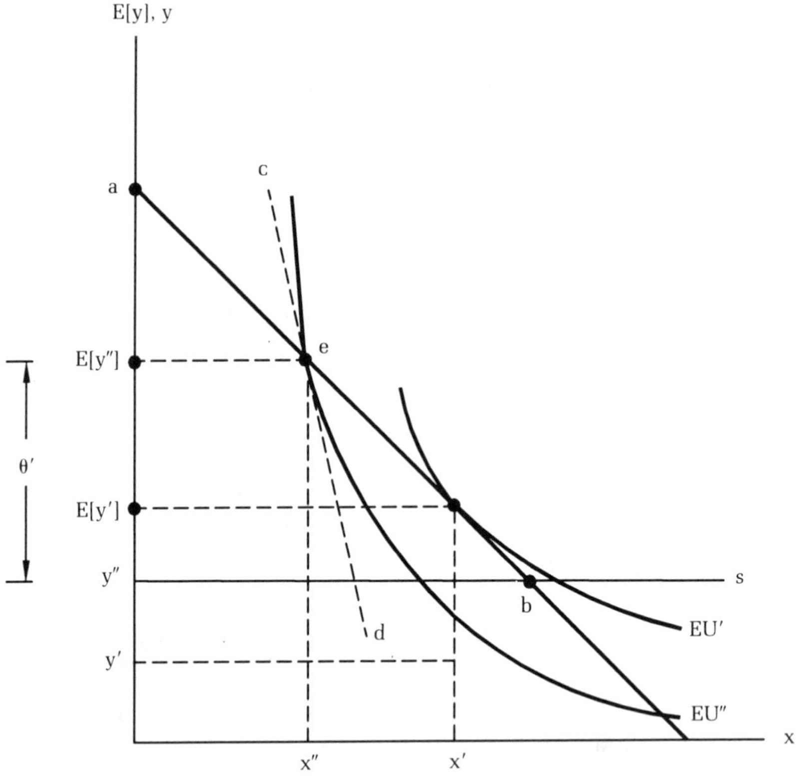

shown in figure 5.3. The household can no longer consume $x'$ because
to do so entails consuming $E[y'] + \theta'$ in the event $\theta'$ is realized,
putting its ex post position below the survivability constraint. Thus,
the household is forced to consume something less than $x'$ of housing
to satisfy the constraint.

By complementary slackness, $\partial L/\partial \lambda = 0$ requires $\lambda > 0$ in (5.44).
Since $\lambda = -dEU/ds > 0$ is the marginal disutility of increasing the
survivability threshold, condition (5.43) requires that $x$ be selected
such that the MRS exceeds the relative market price, or $E[U_x]/E[U_y]$
$> P$. In figure 5.3 the optimal housing level is $x''$, where $E[y''] + \theta'$
$= s$ so that the quantity constraint is binding. The absolute slope of
the expected utility indifference curve $EU''$ at point $e$ exceeds that of
the expected budget line by the amount $\lambda P/E[U_y]$, as required by
condition (5.45). The significance of this condition is that even though

the household is willing to trade off more expected y for additional x than is required by the market, it is precluded from doing so by the quantity constraint.

It is clear from figure 5.3 that relaxing s increases the equilibrium expected welfare level: shifting s downward allows the household to consume more x and to reach a higher expected utility indifference curve (see figure 5.4). Once the constraint falls sufficiently low, though, further decreases have no effect on either housing demand or expected welfare.

More formally, take the total differential of the system (5.43) and $\partial L/\partial \lambda = 0$ and solve using Cramer's Rule to obtain the quantity constraint effect as

$$\partial x/\partial s = -1/P < 0. \tag{5.46}$$

A decrease in s does indeed increase x, as shown in figure 5.4. The constraint modifies housing demand in a quite intuitive fashion. How-

Figure 5.4  CHANGES IN QUANTITY CONSTRAINT

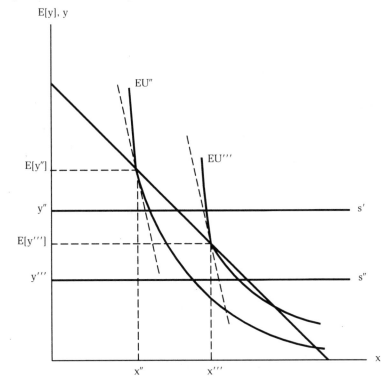

ever, the question remains: Does the quantity constraint alter other demand properties? I now turn to this concern.

### RISK EFFECTS ON MARSHALLIAN HOUSING DEMAND

Solve the differential of the system (5.43) and (5.44) with equality for the increase in mean preserving spread effect as

$$\partial x/\partial \sigma = -x/P < 0. \tag{5.47}$$

Recall that when the quantity constraint is not binding, $\partial x/\partial \sigma$ is determined by two (possibly offsetting) risk effects: the risk income and substitution effects. The former is ambiguous a priori, whereas the latter is unambiguously negative. Result (5.47) demonstrates, however, that the total effect of income uncertainty on housing demand is unambiguously negative under a binding quantity constraint; there is neither an identifiable risk income nor substitution effect. Qualitatively, though, (5.47) still resembles the case where the substitution effect of risk dominates when the quantity constraint is nonbinding.

### MARSHALLIAN DEMAND PROPERTIES

The following results are useful in subsequent analysis. First apply Cramer's Rule for the effect of net income on Marshallian housing demand for the quantity constrained case as

$$\partial x/\partial I^0 = 1/P > 0. \tag{5.48}$$

This result is markedly different from the usual income-effect result. Here, unlike the usual case, increases in income unambiguously increase housing demand, regardless of traditional notions of neutrality or normality. Further, (5.46) and (5.48) reveal

$$\partial x/\partial s = -\partial x/\partial I^0,$$

so that increasing money income has the same effect as decreasing the critical nonhousing consumption value.

Now use Cramer's Rule to solve the total differential of the system, (5.43) and (5.44) with equality, for the housing price effect as

$$\partial x/\partial P = -x/P. \tag{5.49}$$

Looking at (5.48) and (5.49), one finds $\partial x/\partial P = -x(\partial x/\partial I^0)$, and the own-price effect is unambiguously negative. This certainly has intuitive appeal, since any increase in $P$ forces the household to decrease housing demand in order to free up enough ex post purchasing power to allow the attainment of $s$ in state $\theta'$.

LOCATION DEMAND

Having established the properties of the Marshallian housing demand, I can now turn to the issue of location choice under uncertainty and quantity constraint. Substitute $x(P(k), I^0(k);\sigma)$, the solution to (5.41), into the expected utility function and maximize with respect to $k$ to find the optimal location $k^*$ that satisfies

$$-E[U_y]P_k x - E[U_y]T_k + (\partial EU/\partial x)(\partial x/\partial k) = 0. \qquad (5.50)$$

Notice that $\partial L/\partial x = \partial EU/\partial x - \lambda P$ from (5.42), which is zero by (5.43) so that $\partial EU/\partial x = \lambda P$. Substituting for the last term in (5.50) yields

$$E[U_y][-P_k x - T_k] + \lambda P(\partial x/\partial k) = 0. \qquad (5.51)$$

Now, when the quantity constraint is nonbinding, $\lambda = 0$ and (5.51) reduces to Muth's equation, as before. When the constraint is binding, however, $\lambda > 0$, and more manipulation is needed to deal with the third term in (5.51).

To do so, recall $x[P(k), I^0(k);\sigma]$ so that

$$\partial x/\partial k = (\partial x/\partial P)P_k - (\partial x/\partial I^0)T_k. \qquad (5.52)$$

Because $\partial x/\partial P = -x(\partial x/\partial I^0)$ for the quantity constrained case by the application of (5.48) and (5.49), (5.52) reduces to

$$\partial x/\partial k = [-P_k x - T_k](\partial x/\partial I^0). \qquad (5.53)$$

Substituting (5.53) into the last term in (5.51) reveals that

$$E[U_y][-P_k x - T_k] + \lambda P(\partial x/\partial I^0)[-P_k x - T_k] = 0.$$

$$\{E[U_y] + \lambda P(\partial x/\partial I^0)\}[-P_k x - T_k] = 0. \qquad (5.54)$$

But $E[U_y] > 0$ and $\lambda P(\partial x/\partial I^0) > 0$, so that (5.54) reduces to

$$-P_k x - T_k = 0. \qquad (5.55)$$

This, of course, is Muth's equation, from which *the negatively inclined and convex housing price surface result is easily* derived. In addition, (5.55) implies that the bracketed term in (5.53) is zero, so that $\partial x/\partial k = 0$ and *housing demand is constant over those locations where the quantity constraint is binding.*

RISK EFFECTS ON LOCATION AND HOUSING DEMANDS WITH QUANTITY CONSTRAINT

Finally the analysis permits an examination of the effect of income uncertainty on spatial housing demand. An increase in risk lowers housing demand at all locations, shifting the housing demand surface downward. The MBD likewise shifts downward, prodding the household to locate closer to the CBD. Since $\partial x/\partial k = 0$, though, the change in location has no further effect on housing demand, leaving the total effect equal to the direct risk effect, or

$$dk^*/d\sigma = -P_k(\partial x/\partial\sigma)/[P_{kk}x + P_k(\partial x/\partial k) + T_{kk}] < 0$$

$$dx^*/d\sigma = \partial x/\partial\sigma < 0.$$

### OTHER COMPARATIVE STATICS

The comparative static predictions for income, travel costs, and housing price are likewise straightforward under a quantity constraint (see table 5.2 for a summary). All of the total effects on housing demand merely reflect the direct component, since there is no location component in this model (i.e., $\partial x/\partial k = 0$). The effects of price and transportation function changes on location, however, remain ambiguous for those cases where housing price increases (thus reducing MBD) while the slope increases (thus increasing MBD) or where transportation costs increase (thus reducing MBD) while marginal transportation costs also fall (thus reducing MCD).

On the other hand, the taste comparative static results are different in this framework. As before, introduce the taste parameter $\alpha$ into the model such that $\partial x/\partial\alpha > 0$ signifies stronger taste for housing when the quantity constraint is nonbinding. This has no effect on the quantity-constrained equilibrium because the constraint remains $E[y'] + \theta' = s$. In sum, $dx^*/d\alpha = dk^*/d\alpha \equiv 0$ for the quantity constrained household. Small differences in tastes will have no effect on constrained household behavior.

Suppose that instead of examining infinitesimal differences in tastes (as previously described), two households are analyzed that

Table 5.2 COMPARATIVE STATIC EFFECTS UNDER UNCERTAINTY WITH
BINDING QUANTITY CONSTRAINTS

| Increase in: | Sufficient Conditions | Housing $x^*$ | Location $k^*$ |
|---|---|---|---|
| Housing price | $P_{k\alpha} \geq 0$ | — | — |
| | $P_{k\alpha} < 0$ | ? | ? |
| Income | | + | + |
| Commuting costs | $T_{k\alpha} \geq 0$ | — | — |
| | $T_{k\alpha} < 0$ | ? | ? |
| Housing tastes | | 0 | 0 |
| Income risk | Marshallian risk normality | — | — |
| Price risk | Marshallian risk normality | — | — |

exhibit discretely different tastes. Household $A$, for example, has stronger tastes for housing than does household $B$. If one of the households is subject to the binding quantity constraint, it will then be household $A$. Suppose that is the case; applying earlier analysis, household $B$'s housing demand rises with distance, whereas $A$'s is constant, as pictured in the left-hand panel of figure 5.5. Clearly, $MBD^A > MBD^B$ at each $k$ as well, as in the right-hand panel. The implication is straightforward: $k_A > k_B$ and the household with the stronger taste for housing resides farther from the CBD than the otherwise identical household with stronger taste for nonhousing consumption in this case. Thus, *only if the differences in tastes are sufficiently strong to leave one type of household subject to constraint whereas the other is not will stronger tastes for housing translate into more housing consumption and a longer commute.* In any event, the introduction of the quantity constraint fundamentally alters the analysis.

Other questions concerning the introduction of quantity constraints into the theory can be addressed as well. Additional study, though, requires market-level aggregation to incorporate the feedback effect of housing price function changes on household behavior, and so is not pursued further here.

### Uncertain Housing Price Case

The quantity-constrained analysis can similarly be adapted to the uncertain price model in which all of the preceding results can be shown to hold, as in table 5.2.

Figure 5.5 COMPARING HOUSEHOLDS WITH LARGE DIFFERENCES IN TASTES

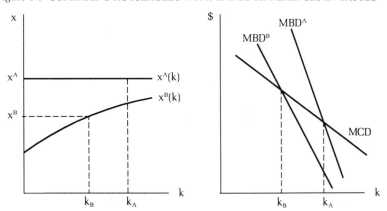

Notes: MDB, marginal benefit of distance; MCD, marginal cost of distance.

### 5.5 UNCERTAIN TRANSPORTATION COSTS

I now extend the model to investigate the relation between uncertain transportation costs and location and housing demands. Following Papageorgiou and Pines (1988), transportation cost uncertainty may arise because households are unsure about how the road and highway system will be maintained or improved during the housing consumption period or about how transportation system congestion will vary in response to ongoing urban development or redevelopment. Transportation cost uncertainty may also be attributable to unpredictability concerning what the household's job site location will be during the housing consumption period, particularly for secondary household workers. This second source of transportation cost uncertainty is particularly relevant when applying the model to multiple employment center urban areas in which household employment may change exogenously from one center to another. In this case, of course, the distance variable, $k$, must be interpreted as the household's effective distance from residence to job site. Nonetheless, the general analysis introduces the stochastic term $\theta$ into the transportation cost function, $T(k;\theta)$, and assumes $T_\theta > 0$, to consider each of the possibilities $T_{k\theta} \lessgtr 0$.

The case in which marginal transportation cost is nonstochastic ($T_{k\theta} = 0$) is particularly straightforward. Since $T(k;\theta) = T(k) + \theta$ in this case, net income is $I^0 = I - T(k) - \theta$, so that the model reduces to the uncertain income formulation in section 5.1. Situations in which the marginal transportation cost is stochastic are a bit more complex, although not quite so complex as the spatially varying price risk case considered earlier. Like that case, though, stochastic marginal transportation cost yields spatially varying risk.

To begin, consider the case where $T_{k\theta} > 0$. This case indicates spatial variation in total transportation cost riskiness, with increasing risk at greater distance from the CBD. The Marshallian housing demand is

$$x[P(k), I^0(k);\sigma] \equiv \text{argmax } EU[x, I - T(k;\theta) - P(k)x].  \quad (5.56)$$

Clearly, (5.56) exhibits the usual properties with respect to price and expected net income (holding risk unchanged). The mean preserving spread effect is found by implicitly differentiating the FOC:

$$\partial x/\partial\sigma = -\{E[U_{xy}T_\theta] - PE[U_{yy}T_\theta]\}/D.  \quad (5.57)$$

Recalling $T_\theta > 0$ and the income-risk comparative statics derivation in chapter 4, (5.57) is identical to the income-risk effect on housing.

Substitute (5.56) into the expected utility function to find the location choice first-order condition (FOC):

$$-E[U_y]P_k x - E[U_y T_k] = 0. \tag{5.58}$$

Since $T_k$ is stochastic, $E[U_y T_k] = E[U_y]E[T_k] + \text{COV}[U_y, T_k]$, so that (5.58) can be rearranged to

$$-P_k x = E[T_k] + \text{COV}[U_y, T_k]/E[U_y]. \tag{5.59}$$

The left-hand term is the marginal change in housing expenditures from moving farther out, denoted MBD as previously. The first term on the right-hand side of the equation is the expected marginal cost of traveling a greater distance to the CBD, whereas the second term is the household's monetized value of the increase or decrease in transportation cost from moving farther out. The expected marginal transportation cost is positive. The marginal risk term, however, takes the sign of the covariance. By direct calculation, $\partial U_y/\partial\theta = -U_{yy}T_\theta > 0$, so that $U_y$ and $\theta$ vary directly. $T_k$ and $\theta$ vary directly (inversely) with one another as $T_{k\theta} \gtrless 0$, which implies that the covariance follows

$$\text{COV}[U_y, T_k] \gtreqless 0 \text{ as } T_{k\theta} \gtreqless 0. \tag{5.60}$$

This result is in keeping with this study's characterization of $T_{k\theta} \gtrless 0$ as indicating spatially increasing (decreasing) transportation cost risk.

Only in the case where $T_{k\theta} = 0$ does (5.59) reduce to the usual statement of Muth's equation. More generally, when $T_{k\theta} \geq 0$, the second term is non-negative so that the entire RHS of (5.59) is positive, implying $P_k < 0$. Alternatively, when $T_{k\theta} < 0$, $P_k$ can take any sign.

The approach here follows that taken to analyze spatial variation in price risk. I evaluate transportation cost-risk effects on housing and location sequentially, breaking total risk into risk level and spatial variation components. Consider figure 5.6. Beginning with no spatial variation in risk, an increase in transportation cost uncertainty reduces housing demand $x(k)$ to $x(k)'$, prodding the household to reduce travel distance from $k_1$ to $k_3$. The reduction in distance increases housing price (recall that I begin from a point at which $T_{k\theta} = 0$ and introduce spatial variation in risk later). The increase in price prompts the household to further reduce housing from $x_2$ to $x_3$, reinforcing the direct risk effect of $x_1$ to $x_2$ to yield a total change in housing demand $x_1$ to $x_3$.

Now introduce spatially increasing transportation cost risk ($T_{k\theta} > 0$). In figure 5.6, increasing risk on the margin is introduced at $\{x_3, k_3\}$: the spatial risk component of MCD shifts the relevant curve

Figure 5.6  SPATIALLY INCREASING TRANSPORTATION COST RISK EFFECTS ON
          HOUSING AND LOCATION DEMANDS

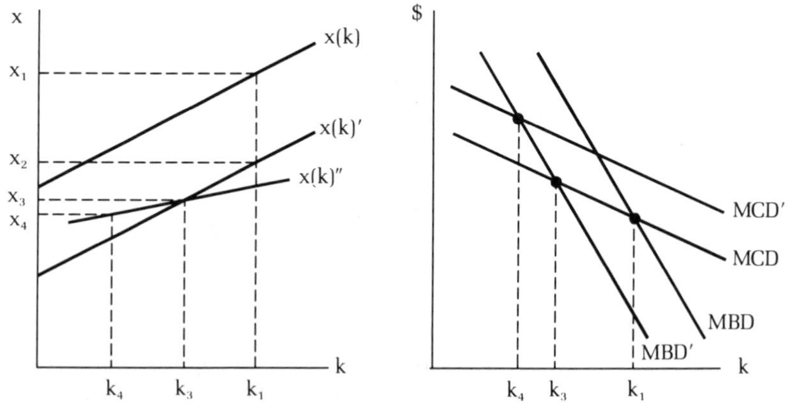

Notes: MDB, marginal benefit of distance; MCD, marginal cost of distance.

to MCD$'$, reducing optimal commuting distance to $k_4$. The spatial risk
component rotates the housing demand gradient from $x(k)'$ to $x(k)''$ in
the figure, because distances greater than $k_3$ entail increasing risk and
reduced housing demand, whereas distances less than $k_3$ entail decreasing risk and greater housing demand. (Notice that MBD$'$ steepens
as well, even though it is not shown in the figure.) The shift in MCD
and rotation in $x(k)$ induced by spatial risk further reduces optimal
distance and housing demand, to $k_4$ and $x_4$, respectively.

Alternatively, spatially decreasing transportation cost risk ($T_{k\theta} < 0$)
offsets the risk level effect. As in the preceding case, an increase in
risk level by itself shifts the curve $x(k)$ to $x(k)'$ and MBD to MBD$'$,
prompting the household to reside closer to the CBD ($k_3$) where it
consumes less housing ($x_3$). The introduction of spatially decreasing
risk shifts MCD to MCD$'$ and reinforces a steeper housing demand
gradient ($x[k]'$ to $x[k]''$): the additional effect of spatial variation in
transportation cost risk is to offset the effect of risk level on location
and housing demand.

In summary, *transportation cost uncertainty, like income uncertainty, increases the demand for proximity while reducing housing
demand. Spatially increasing risk reinforces this result, whereas spatially decreasing risk offsets it.* This partial equilibrium analysis
therefore relates well to the market-level study by Papageorgiou and
Pines (1988). Their model focuses on how transportation cost uncertainty affects equilibrium land rent and residential density in the
closed monocentric city. Consistent with the results here, they argue

that such uncertainty steepens the household's bid rent, reflecting greater demand for proximity, leading to a more compact city wherein households enjoy a lower level of expected utility in equilibrium.[2] As asserted at the outset, I generally expected to find similar partial equilibrium and market equilbrium results, which in this case were confirmed.

---

### 5.6 UNCERTAIN HOUSING QUALITY

This section of the study extends the location demand model by formally addressing complications introduced by uncertain housing quality, closely following the partial equilibrium modeling in Turnbull (1991). This model depicts consumers making housing consumption commitments without certain knowledge about how a specific combination of land, capital, and location translate into housing consumption ex post. The consumption risk envisioned here may be caused by one or more of several factors whose effects are not known beforehand: the housing unit's structural design, or how well floor plans actually work for the individual family's life-style; workmanship embodied in the structure itself; and neighborhood effects, or how the surrounding land use or development patterns affect the level of housing services obtained from the given house-lot combination and the effect of neighbors' life-styles on the family's enjoyment of its own housing package. The household has rational expectations and recognizes the various possibilities that may be realized ex post.

The innovation of this model is the formal introduction of uncertainty over housing quality. The consumer makes location and consumption decisions prior to knowing with certainty the quantity of housing services that will be extracted from the quantity of housing purchased. For what follows I define $z$ as housing purchased or planned consumption and $x$ as actual or ex post housing consumption. All other notation remains as in previous sections. The relationship between purchased and ex post consumption is specified as

$$x = \theta z, \tag{5.61}$$

where $\theta > 0$ is a stochastic term with mean one and finite variance. The stochastic term captures the consumer's uncertainty over housing quality when making purchase and location decisions.

The risk-averse consumer's problem is to maximize expected utility subject to (5.61) and the usual budget constraint. Following the now familiar procedure, solve the budget constraint for $y$ and substitute the resultant expression and (5.61) into the expected utility function to obtain $EU[\theta z, I^0 - P(k)z]$. The first stage of the household's optimization problem is to find the optimal *planned* housing consumption at a given distance $k$:

$$z(P, I^0;\sigma) \equiv \text{argmax } EU[\theta z, I - T(k) - P(k)z], \qquad (5.62)$$

where $I^0 = I - T(k)$ and $\sigma$ is again a parameter reflecting the level of consumption riskiness for given $z$.

The planned housing demand satisfies the FOC

$$E[U_x;\theta] - E[U_y]P(k) = 0,$$

which yields the uncertainty analogue to the usual consumer equilibrium condition,

$$E[U_x\theta]/E[U_y] = P(k).$$

The optimal consumption bundle is where the expected marginal rate of substitution between housing and nonhousing consumption, $MRS_{x,y}$, equals the relative price ratio.

## Planned Housing Demand Gradient and Housing Price Function

Concerning the choice of residential location, the consumer considers each of the budget constraints available at different distances, selecting the constraint corresponding to the location yielding the greatest expected utility. Mathematically, substitute (5.62) into the expected utility function to obtain the indirect expected utility function

$$\Phi[P(k), I - T(k);\sigma] = EU[\theta z(P, I^0;\sigma), I^0 - Pz(P, I^0;\sigma)]. \quad (5.63)$$

The optimal location $k^*$ satisfies the FOC

$$-E[U_y]P_k z(P, I^0;\sigma) - E[U_y]T_k = 0,$$

which reduces to

$$-P_k z(P, I^0;\sigma) - T_k = 0, \qquad (5.64)$$

clearly recognizable as Muth's equation with minor modification. This condition again requires that $P_k < 0$ and *housing price declines with greater effective distance from the CBD, as in the certainty model.* Given $P_k < 0$, condition (5.64) therefore requires that the household locate where the marginal benefit of moving farther away from the CBD, in the form of savings on *planned* housing expenditures $-P_k z$, equals the marginal cost of distance, $T_k$.

From the second-order condition (SOC) for location choice, the result is

$$-P_{kk}z(P, I^0;\sigma) - (\partial z/\partial k)P_k - T_{kk} < 0. \tag{5.65}$$

Since the last term is nonpositive by specification, $P_k < 0$ from (5.64) and $(\partial z/\partial k) > 0$, as shown below, $P_{kk} > 0$ must hold for (5.65) to hold, and *housing price is decreasing convex in distance—as in the certainty model and the uncertainty formulations considered earlier.*

I now use the important demand properties for the quality uncertainty case established in section 4.5 to consider the spatial variation in planned housing demand. Differentiate (5.62) with respect to distance to find

$$\begin{aligned}
(\partial z/\partial k) &= (\partial z/\partial P)P_k - (\partial z/\partial I^0)T_k \\
&= (\partial z/\partial P)P_k + (\partial z/\partial I^0)P_k z \\
&= [(\partial Z/\partial P) - z(\partial z/\partial I^0)]P_k + (\partial z/\partial I^0)P_k z \\
&= (\partial Z/\partial P)P_k > 0,
\end{aligned} \tag{5.66}$$

where the second line follows from $T_k = -P_k z$ by (5.64), the third follows by application of the Slutsky equation (see section 4.5), and the fourth by application of the Substitution Theorem and $P_k < 0$. *The optimal level of planned housing consumption therefore increases with distance, another result qualitatively consistent with the usual depiction.*

## Consumption Risk Effects

As before, the optimal planned housing consumption is found by substituting $k^*$ into (5.62) to obtain

$$z^* = z[P(k^*), I - T(k^*, I);\sigma]. \tag{5.67}$$

The effect of a mean-preserving increase in quality risk (denoted $d\sigma > 0$) is found by implicit differentiation of (5.64):

$$dk^*/d\sigma = (\partial z/\partial \sigma)E[U_y]P_k/\Phi_{kk}. \tag{5.68}$$

Direct differentiation of (5.67) reveals the risk effect on optimal planned housing consumption as

$$dz^*/d\sigma = (\partial z/\partial \sigma) + (\partial z/\partial k)(dk^*/d\sigma). \tag{5.69}$$

The partial derivative $\partial z/\partial\sigma$ is the direct effect of risk on Marshallian housing demand holding location unchanged; the second term in (5.69) is the indirect or location effect of risk on housing demand.

Because increased riskiness lowers housing demand in the nonspatial uncertainty model under the conditions explained in section 4.5, $(\partial z/\partial\sigma) < 0$, $dk^*/d\sigma < 0$, and $dz^*/d\sigma < 0$ as well: *the household responds to quality risk by reducing planned housing consumption and residing closer to the CBD.* Intuitively, the risk lowers housing demand at each location (the direct effect or first term in [5.69]), which lowers the housing expenditure savings obtained by moving farther out. Graphically, the housing consumption gradient in figure 5.7's left-hand panel shifts downward, with the concomitant decrease in MBD in the right-hand panel as well. The lower marginal benefit of distance prods the household to reside closer to the CBD, from $k_1$ to $k_3$. But the decrease in distance also prompts the household to lower housing consumption via the location effect, $z_2$ to $z_3$, (the second term in [5.69]), reinforcing the direct effect on housing demand, $z_1$ to $z_2$.

Although not immediately obvious, another interesting regularity between nonspatial and spatial demand theories is observed in this model. Equations (5.66) and (5.68) and the Slutsky equation can be applied to restate (5.69) as

$$dz^*/d\sigma = (\partial z/\partial\sigma) + (\partial z/\partial\sigma)\{(\partial Z/\partial P)P_k^2 E[U_y]\}/\Phi_{kk}. \qquad (5.70)$$

The term in brackets is positive by the Substitution Theorem for the quality risk case, implying that the indirect or location effect of risk

Figure 5.7  QUALITY RISK EFFECTS ON HOUSING AND LOCATION

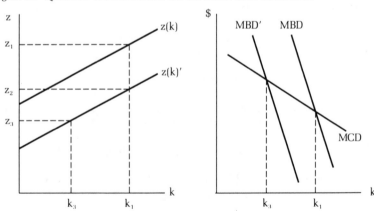

Notes: MDB, marginal benefit of distance; MCD, marginal cost of distance.

will always reinforce the direct effect. The total effect of quality risk-iness on location will be entirely determined by the sign of the Mar-shallian comparative static result $(\partial z/\partial \sigma)$. Thus, even if the conditions derived in chapter 4 do not pertain and the intuitively perverse Mar-shallian risk effect $\partial z/\partial \sigma > 0$ is observed, location and spatial housing demand comparative statics will nonetheless always follow the non-spatial Marshallian outcome.

## Other Comparative Statics

The comparative static predictions summarized in table 5.1 for loca-tion and housing demand responses to changes in income, housing price, transportation costs, and tastes are found using (5.64) and (5.67). It can be shown that greater incomes, lower transportation costs, or stronger tastes for housing increase the marginal benefit of distance (MBD) and therefore move the household's optimal location farther from the CBD while increasing planned consumption. A steeper housing price function slope reinforces the downward shift in the MBD curve in a diagram like figure 5.1, reinforcing the outward movement of residence location and the increase in housing demand. A shallower price slope tends to offset the increase in MBD, thus offsetting these location and housing demand effects.

A decrease in the marginal cost of distance (MCD) due to a shal-lower travel cost function shifts the MCD curve downward in figure 5.1, also reinforcing the outward household movement and greater housing demand effect of a decrease in travel costs. An increase in the slope of the travel cost function, on the other hand, increases the MCD, shifting MCD upwards in figure 5.1. This shift offsets the out-ward movement and housing demand increase induced by lower transportation costs.

---

## 5.7 STOCHASTIC TASTES AND PREFERENCES

Before concluding, consider an alternative interpretation of the pre-vious sets of results. Assume for the sake of illustration that $\theta$ in the model explained in the previous section can take only one of two values, say $1 + \epsilon$ and $1 - \epsilon$, where $\epsilon$ is some positive constant. Assume $0 < \epsilon < 1$ to ensure that $\theta > 0$ holds for all possible outcomes. The introduction of stochastic quality into the model leaves the consumer with state-dependent indifference maps, that is, with a different set of indifference maps for each realizable value of $\theta$.

Suppose that the consumer selects consumption bundle $[z^0 \ y^0]$. If the realization of $\theta = 1 + \epsilon$, the consumer will enjoy utility $U^1 = U(z^0(1 + \epsilon), y^0)$. If the realization of $\theta = 1 - \epsilon$, then the consumer will enjoy utility $U^2 = U(z^0(1 - \epsilon), y^0)$ ex post, where $U^1$ and $U^2$ are indifference curves from completely different indifference curve "families" or maps, generated by $U[z(1 + \epsilon), y]$ and $U[z(1 - \epsilon), y]$, respectively. When evaluated at a given consumption bundle, greater realized values of $\theta$ clearly lower the marginal rate of substitution between housing and nonhousing consumption ex post; the $MRS_{x,y}$ at $[z^0 \ y^0]$ in state $\theta = 1 - \epsilon$ on $U^2$ is less than that in state $\theta = 1 + \epsilon$ on $U^1$. Intuitively, the effect of $\theta$ on ex post indifference maps is the same as the effect of a change in tastes on indifference curves in the certainty model (DeSalvo 1977b; Muth 1969). Mathematically, the introduction of the consumption risk via the $\theta$ term in the model mathematically operates much like a shift parameter, rotating and shifting the ex post indifference map describing the ordinal rankings of planned housing consumption $z$ and nonhousing consumption $y$.

If one interprets the $\theta$ term as a "housing taste" parameter, then the preceding analysis of uncertain housing quality also relates directly to the model of consumer behavior when tastes are uncertain ex ante. A high realization of $\theta$, for example, would indicate relatively weaker tastes for housing, since the consumer obviously obtains more enjoyment (or effective housing consumption) out of a given level of housing purchased. A low realization of $\theta$, to continue, would then indicate relatively stronger tastes for housing, since the consumer obtains less enjoyment out of a given level of housing purchased.[3]

With this alternative interpretation of $\theta$, what do the preceding results imply? Under the stipulated conditions, greater $\theta$ risk—whatever the interpretation—leads to increased demand for CBD proximity and decreased demand for housing. Thus, I arrive at the seemingly paradoxical result that households whose evolution of preferences over the consumption period for their housing purchase is more uncertain will have a lower demand for housing. Although this may seem wrong at first, this conclusion does have intuitive appeal upon reflection. The key insight is to remember that greater uncertainty over future tastes for housing is symmetric: there is a probability of weaker tastes for housing as well as a probability of stronger tastes for housing. It is the potential ex post utility penalty of "overconsuming" housing that increases with the uncertainty, thus dampening housing demand ex ante.

---

### 5.8 CONCLUDING REMARKS

This chapter has presented a partial equilibrium model of housing and location demand under uncertainty. A key assumption underlying our results is that housing represents inflexible consumption that cannot be readily altered in response to fluctuations in income, price, consumption services, transportation costs, or even consumer tastes. Taken together, the results show that different sources of risks affect housing and location demands in different ways. In addition, the spatial characteristics of risk are also seen to affect consumer housing and location demands in intuitively appealing and predictable fashion.

Regarding the contribution of this approach to the method of uncertainty analysis, early attempts in the literature had difficulty deriving and providing meaningful and intuitive economic interpretations of results. Following and extending the approaches taken in a series of recent studies, though, I discovered a mode of analysis capable of demonstrating how standard nonspatial uncertainty demand theory can be exploited to more easily derive and understand the spatial demand theory under uncertainty. The fact that spatial demand behavior can be characterized directly from received nonspatial theory is the common thread of chapter 2. The extension of this relationship to the uncertainty environment in this chapter clearly demonstrates how spatial uncertainty theory can be made more readily tractable and related directly to nonspatial uncertainty theory.

Other dimensions of the urban consumer's choice process need to be addressed in the context of income and price uncertainty. Integrating the investment motives for acquiring owner-occupied housing with the financing complications are two nontrivial tasks that have not received adequate attention in location demand theory; the user-cost approach taken here is abstract and neglects explicit treatment of the role of housing in household investment portfolio decisions. Nonetheless, the theory presented here coupled with the work of Henderson and Ioannides (1983) provides the foundation for additional work in this direction; the principles of location demand under income and price uncertainty established in this chapter will prove essential to understanding how these complicating factors affect housing and location demand.

Turning to the empirical ramifications of the theory, a variety of uncertainties as well as spatial variations in risks affect housing and location demands. Empirical evidence supporting the theoretical predictions for the effect of income uncertainty on housing demand has been presented by Haurin and Gill (1987). More empirical work is needed, especially empirical studies explicitly addressing the location demand effects of income, price, and quality uncertainty, extending perhaps along the lines of the empirical study of certainty location theory by Blackley and Follain (1987). Still, even though the theory reveals that measures of overall levels and spatial variations in risks need to be included in empirical specifications of housing and location demands in order to avoid specification bias, I cannot predict how empirically important the neglected effects will be. Further, finding appropriate empirical proxies for these factors will be difficult. But here, too, is where additional theoretical development is necessary, to tie theoretical risk factors to observable characteristics of urban labor and housing markets.

---

### Notes

1. In the uncertainty analysis I examine differential effects of changes in $\beta$ from zero; hence, the covariance term is properly evaluated at infinitesimal $\beta$ in the neighborhood of zero, conditional upon location equilibrium $k$. The covariance term is positive when $\delta + \beta k$ is positive. The sign of the covariance term follows from the properties of similar-dissimilar orderings, using $\partial U_y / \partial \theta > 0$.

2. These results are conditional upon introducing a "small" level of risk into the certainty model under the assumption of the "principle of decreasing risk aversion to concentration." Not surprisingly, though, this assumption is closely related to the "risk normality" notion employed in the partial equilibrium analysis here.

3. Viewed somewhat differently, the high-$\theta$ consumer would choose less housing consumption ex post than the low-$\theta$ consumer. In this sense, the latter has stronger tastes for housing. This may seem at odds with the fact that the high-$\theta$ consumer obtains a larger marginal utility of housing than the low-$\theta$ consumer, except when one notices that the ex post choice (if it could be made, that is) is consistent with this study's earlier characterization of different housing tastes because the high-$\theta$ consumer has a lower $MRS_{z,y}$ than his or her low-$\theta$ counterpart.

# Chapter Six

# CONCLUSION

This study has presented a complete treatment of urban consumer theory, from the simplest models through major variants dealing with non-CBD employment, labor/leisure choice, local taxes and government services, as well as various types of uncertainty, ranging from income risk to housing quality risk. Some of the models have been long established in the urban economics literature, whereas others are more recent. The derived results are themselves of direct interest; the variety of models gives remarkably robust comparative static predictions under conditions of both certainty and uncertainty. The analysis demonstrates the spatial change in housing demand patterns that ultimately drives market-level changes. At the market level of analysis, of course, the price function adjusts endogenously to the spatial changes in housing demand by the various types of consumers. Still, existing aggregate models typically reveal comparative statics that reflect the types of changes derived in the partial equilibrium theory here; it can be shown that endogenous changes in the house price function do not normally overshadow the initial consumer response to income, transportation costs, or taste changes in the certainty model. Thus, the comparative statics derived throughout this study give at the least a useful first approximation of how housing and location choices will ultimately work themselves out at the market level.

In addition to the particular derived results, and perhaps more important, this study contributes to method. Housing exhibits certain unique characteristics when compared with other goods: it is heterogeneous, particularly in the spatial dimension, and housing consumption is tied to a highly durable asset that is difficult to adjust to short-term variations in prices and incomes. The spatial heterogeneity is dealt with in urban consumer theory by explicitly addressing the choice of residential location undertaken by the consumer. The approach to urban consumer theory employed throughout this study emphasizes the connection between standard nonspatial consumer theory and the spatial consumer theory that forms the core micro-foundation in urban and real estate economics. This approach has several advantages. First, the role of nonspatial demand theory in urban consumer theory is clarified by decomposing comparative statics into two components, identified as the direct effect on housing demand and the indirect or location effect on housing demand, the latter of which captures how housing demand varies as the consumer optimally changes his or her location. The decomposition into direct and indirect effects emphasizes how nonspatial comparative statics are modified by the introduction of location choice in the consumer theory; it also simplifies the interpretation of results by expressing mathematical conditions in terms of nonspatial demand concepts easily recognized by the nonspecialist with some background in standard microeconomics.

Second, the modeling approach taken in this study simplifies the derivation of comparative statics, allowing one to avoid often messy determinant expansions and mathematical conditions that appear more obscure than economically intuitive. Third, the method lends itself to easy graphical derivations and interpretations of all results.

The other properties of housing, durability and high transactions costs, require the introduction of uncertainty, since consumers must make their fixed housing decisions before they know with certainty how various economic factors ranging from employment to property taxes will evolve during the consumption period. Chapters 4 and 5 integrated the spatial heterogeneity and durability properties of housing into the consumer model by examining the housing and location choice theory under conditions of uncertainty. As in the earlier chapters dealing with decisions under certainty, the approach emphasized the links between nonspatial uncertainty theory and spatial uncertainty theory by decomposing housing demand comparative statics into direct and indirect or location components. Here again, the analytical and pedagogical values of this approach were demonstrated; it makes complicated analysis considerably simpler, economically intuitive, and amenable to graphical derivation and explanation.

# COMMENTATOR'S REMARKS

The AREUEA Monograph Committee, in consultation with monograph authors, selects outside commentators to provide suggestions to the author in making revisions to the manuscript. In addition, commentators are asked to provide brief remarks on aspects of the literature that may not be fully covered in the main text. Commentators are selected based on their area of expertise and on their published research.

Two sets of commentators' remarks were solicited for this monograph. The first commentary, by James Follain, places the study of urban consumer theory within the general context of a well taught course in urban economics. The decentralization of residences and jobs ranks high among the list of "stylized facts" which research in real estate and urban economics has tried to explain. Urban consumer theory provides the basis for explaining these phenomena. Indeed, the challenge facing researchers is to make their empirical testing consistent with the restrictions on behavior suggested by the theory. Finally Follain notes the further challenge of making the effects of uncertainty as modeled in urban consumer theory consistent with models of the stochastic city that use option theory to explain stylized facts about development at the urban fringe.

The second set of remarks, by C. F. Sirmans, reinforces Follain's call for empirical work that is capable of testing the rich implications of urban consumer theory. Specifically, Sirmans notes that there may be an association between the level of income and income uncertainty or between occupational categories and income uncertainty. Such associations have implications for spatial patterns of settlement by various groups that should be tested.

# SOME ADDITIONAL MOTIVATION FOR INCORPORATING SPACE INTO THE THEORY OF THE CONSUMER

James R. Follain

Geoffrey Turnbull's monograph is an excellent contribution to an important component of urban economics. Long-time urban economists as well as newcomers to the field will benefit from the book's consistent, concise, and well-written discussion. Graduate students in economics making the transition from the basic microeconomic theory of the consumer to urban economics will especially appreciate Turnbull's elucidation of the linkage between consumer location theory and the standard theory of the consumer.

In works of this type, a certain tension always exists over the relative emphasis given to theoretical development versus motivational theory. Turnbull chose to err on the side of consistent theoretical presentation; whereas some of the motivational theory is presented in the text, much of it is contained in the study's numerous citations.

Given Turnbull's choice and my own work in this regard, my comments here stress the broader context of this monograph for those new to the field. Three areas especially merit additional discussion: the motivation for the study of urban economics; the need for and complexity of empirical work on consumer location; and other ways to account for uncertainty in an urban model.

## MOTIVATION

Urban economics has long sought to understand the relative decline in the size and composition of central cities within the United States and elsewhere in the world. Many researchers refer to this as the decentralization or "suburbanization" of urban areas. The primary policy question in this connection within the United States is whether the suburbanization represents a "flight from blight" or, as many urban economists have argued, a natural outcome of economic and technological progress in a free society.

Among numerous discussions of this issue and its importance to urban economics, one particularly effective essay is that by Mieszkowski and Mills (1993). The authors categorize the contributions of economists to the suburbanization debate since the 1940s and examine the two major explanations for this phenomenon. The first they label the "natural evolution theory," which stresses the importance of economic growth and transportation improvements as causes of suburbanization. The second is often referred to as a "flight from blight" theory of decentralization, according to which people have fled central cities because of the many social and fiscal ills that plague these areas, including high property taxes, high crime rates, racial tensions, and more. A reading of Mieszkowski and Mills's essay prior to Turnbull's study will enhance one's understanding of Turnbull's and others' work. Chapter 2 of the monograph is especially relevant to the natural evolution theory, and chapter 3 is most closely tied to flight from blight theories.

An appreciation for the motivation for studying consumer location theory can also be obtained by considering a number of stylized facts that modern urban economics seeks to explain. I present such a list in both my graduate and undergraduate urban classes, and although the elements and ordering of items vary from year to year, the exercise helps both the students and me remain focused on the central tenets of urban economics. The following is a condensed list of stylized facts about urban areas that are better grasped by introducing "space" into the basic microeconomic theory of the consumer. Some can be easily linked to the Turnbull text and some require more effort, but all are better understood by a careful reading of the monograph.

1. *Population and housing densities decline with distance from the central business district (CBD) at a decreasing rate.* Clearly, suburban areas tend to be less densely populated than central parts of metropolitan areas. What may be surprising to most, however, is that these densities tend to decline at a decreasing rate and that the negative exponential function often fits the pattern quite well. This information helps to illuminate the importance of Turnbull's discussion in chapter 2, especially equation (2.5) and the "Housing Price Function" subsection of section 2.1.

2. *Urban population and housing densities have declined over time and among other countries in addition to the United States.* Many people perceive of suburbanization as a post–World War II and largely U.S. phenomenon. Urban economists have shown clearly that this is

not the case. The decentralization of U.S. cities began well before World War II. There is some controversy about the beginning of this decline, but Mieszkowski and Mills's (1993) review suggests that the "most rapid period of suburbanization as measured by the change in the density gradient occurred between 1920 and 1950" (1993: 140). These authors also survey evidence indicating that the pattern of decentralization is found in many other countries as well. In this regard, one of Muth's (1969) key contributions was to show how urban economic theory can be used to develop and test numerous hypotheses regarding the shape of the population and price gradients. The comparative statics presented by Turnbull in the "Housing Price Function" subsection of section 2.1 are the basis for many of these tests.

3. *Higher-income households tend to live farther from the CBD.* This is an issue that has long attracted the attention of urban economists. Few doubt the validity of the stylized fact, but many debate whether the standard urban model is capable of explaining it. The answer depends critically upon the parameters of the consumer's utility function. Although Turnbull discusses some of this debate, I recommend that students read the original articles. I found the debate fascinating and quite helpful in my initial study of urban economics nearly 20 years ago. It inspired a paper by Steven Malpezzi and me (1981) in which we offered tests of the standard urban model versus the "blight flight" model. Our work, as well as my own reading of the evidence, suggests that suburbanization is a complex phenomenon and that both models are needed to understand it.

4. *Employment is becoming more decentralized as well.* Whether jobs follow people or people follow jobs is another central question in urban economics. More than likely, the two are simultaneously determined. The emergence of "edge cities" in so many major metropolitan areas poses another and related challenge.[1] An additional aspect of this issue concerns "spatial mismatch," which refers to the possibility that high unemployment among many inner-city black youths stems from an increasing separation between their residences (central cities) and the location of jobs (suburbs).[2] Some recent literature has attempted to discuss more general notions of the separation of inner-city communities from the rest of the urban area (e.g., Galster and Killen 1994). Understanding the causes and consequences of such separation ought to be a high priority of consumer location theory.

5. *Racial disparities exist between cities and suburbs.* This fact may be more apparent in the United States than in other countries, but it is an issue that ought to be addressed by models of consumer location theory. The extent of the disparities has been described and analyzed

by many urban economists and others, including a recent and thorough review by Frey and Fielding (1994). Yinger and others have demonstrated on numerous occasions the importance of incorporating this issue into the standard urban model. It can lead to significant distortions in the shape of the urban gradients, and any complete model of consumer location choice in the United States should take it into account.

Some important issues have probably been omitted from this list, and those cited may be more questionable than the term *stylized facts* suggests. Nevertheless, a list like this can lead to interesting interactions between students and teachers, in addition to contributing to an appreciation of the models described by Turnbull.

---

## EMPIRICAL RESEARCH ON CONSUMER LOCATION

In chapter 1, Turnbull asks: "Why Partial Equilibrium Analysis?" His answer is a good one, but, in my view, it understates an important part of the answer. A partial equilibrium model of consumer location theory is needed to guide empirical work regarding such behavior. Just as we estimate models of food consumption, clothing consumption and housing consumption, we need models to explain where people choose to consume such goods, especially housing. We also need to estimate models that explain where people work in relation to where they live. Theory such as that offered by Turnbull ought to offer insights, hypotheses, and restrictions to guide such work.

As Turnbull mentions, empirical work along these lines is scant. Much work has been done to estimate housing demand equations, but few authors incorporate both location and housing choice. A study by Dixie Blackley and me (1987), cited by Turnbull, made such an attempt, using microdata and estimating a reduced form equation for both housing and residential location. This work offers some basic support for the standard urban model, but it also reveals the difficulty of testing the urban model. We originally set out to estimate the first-order conditions (the structural model) underlying consumer location choice as represented by the first-order condition for locational equilibrium. We discovered, however, that even the most elementary test of this hypothesis required numerous assumptions, and severe restrictions had to be placed on the sample. Despite these steps, we were unable to produce meaningful results regarding the locational equilibrium condition. In fact, the consumer model put forth by Turnbull is extremely demanding in data. To test it requires, for example, information about the shape of the housing price function at the residence of the household, the speed of travel to and from work, and more. A real-world test of the model also requires information about the cost and benefits to consumers of travel to other points of interest such as shopping and entertainment. Measurement of these variables is rare and difficult; as a consequence, tests of the consumer location models with microdata are rare and difficult under the best of circumstances.

Hamilton (1982) used a creative approach to test elements of the standard urban model. He asked whether households commute excessively in studies where the predictions of the standard urban model are used as the standard of comparison. He found that they do. Other analysts have produced results that are less harsh on the urban model. Regardless, the point remains that relatively little empirical evidence exists to support the standard urban model, especially some of its specific first-order conditions. The evidence that does exist is often obtained using aggregate data of one sort or another, such as that presented by Muth (1985) to explain variations in density gradients or by Hamilton (1982) in analyzing aggregate commuting patterns. More work is needed, and theorists like Turnbull are helping to show how the theory can be used to generate testable hypotheses.

---

## UNCERTAINTY

As Turnbull states, his discussion of the role of uncertainty emphasizes the newest work in urban consumer location theory. The theory is still largely taught and practiced as a theory with certainty. In this connection, his careful treatment of the basic theory of consumer choice under uncertainty is instructive in its own right and an important prerequisite to his chapter 5. Turnbull's characterization of uncertainty follows logically from the foundations of consumer location choice presented in the preceding chapters.

Another strand of literature introduces uncertainty into the urban model somewhat differently and in a way I find more compelling. This literature builds upon the work of Capozza and Helsley (1989) and others, focusing on urban growth in which there is uncertainty regarding the expansion of future income and population and, hence, land prices. Real estate developers with vacant urban land must decide when to develop it and how much to invest. Once the investment is made, it is not easily reversed. A key outcome of this theory is a condition in which the investment decision depends upon the "option" value of the real estate. If the investment is made today, then the investor forgoes the option of investing differently in the future. As such, the expected investment return in real estate development must actually exceed the return available on other investments that are otherwise comparable in risk and expected return. Among its other virtues, this model is capable of explaining an important stylized fact (one I did not include on the preceding list)—why the price of land at the urban fringe tends to exceed the present value of future agricultural rents associated with such land. The answer, according to the theory, is that the price of land includes the option value of the real estate as well as the present value of the agricultural rents.

Another interesting aspect of this literature is its clear linkage to the modern theory of financial economics and, in particular, to option pricing theory. The option value of urban land is shown to depend upon the expected volatility of population and income growth, the exogenous variables that ultimately determine land value. Greater uncertainty, all else equal, increases both the value of the option and the value of the land. These comparative statics are familiar to students of financial economics in their study of the comparative statics of the values of stock and bond options.

Modern financial economics has shown the importance of incorporating uncertainty into models of financial markets. I applaud the work of Turnbull, Capozza and Helsley, and others in integrating uncertainty into the study of urban life. I suspect we will find it no less important in urban economics than it has been in financial economics.

---

### Notes

1. The term *edge city*, popularized by Joel Garreau in *Edge City* (New York: Doubleday, 1991), refers to the large clusters of populations and jobs located on the edges of metropolitan areas.

2. The spatial mismatch literature is large; one recent summary is found in Holzer (1991).

# FURTHER IMPLICATIONS OF UNCERTAINTY THEORY

C. F. Sirmans

Consumer location choice has been analyzed for over three decades, yet many issues still remain unresolved in the literature. Geoffrey Turnbull has undertaken a major task, synthesizing an extensive literature with detailed mathematical and graphical derivations of important insights. The depth of coverage in such a short presentation makes the monograph useful as either a textbook or an instructional guide. Because the monograph focuses on partial equilibrium consumer theory alone, it can be used as a supplementary source of background information for textbooks that tend to focus on the market level of analysis.

The organization of the material helps to clarify the structure of the established theories and their interrelatedness, while dividing the broad topic of "urban consumer theory" into manageable segments. The inclusion of the new and growing literature on uncertainty analysis is, I think, a particularly important contribution. This is an area of study that will move us closer to a successful merger between the urban economics paradigm of location choice and the real estate finance paradigm of investment.

Even though the uncertainty theory discussed in the text covers much ground, it is important to examine additional implications of the theory. Some of my examples are based upon the work of Henderson and Ioannides (1983) and Turnbull et al. (1991), and some are simple applications or extensions of what is presented in the text.

Consider some empirical implications of the income risk theory that were not cited in the text. It is safe to assume that the labor market of a given urban area is segmented between blue-collar and white-collar employment, with blue-collar wages typically lower than white-collar earnings. The "Comparative Statics" subsection of section 2.1 argues that white-collar workers prefer to live farther away from their jobs than do blue-collar workers. However, until the mid-1980s, blue-collar workers generally faced a greater risk of layoff or termination from plant closure than their white-collar counterparts. Nevertheless, as the "Income Risk Effects" subsection of section 5.1 demonstrates, greater income risk from layoff or terminations by itself tends to increase blue-collar workers' demand for central business district (CBD) accessibility relative to that of white-collar workers. The employment risk for blue-collar workers, therefore, tends to reinforce the location demand effects of their relatively lower income, reducing blue-collar housing demand and increasing CBD accessibility. It is clear, therefore, how income risk can be an additional relevant factor unaccounted for in the income-location debate summarized in the "Comparative Statics" subsection of section 2.1. Even if our income elasticity and marginal cost of distance estimates suggest at best a weak tendency for spatial segregation by income level (as found by Wheaton [1977b]), the overlooked risk factors can provide the marginal location demand differences leading to the patterns observed across urban areas.

Continuing with my example, from about the mid-1980s, white-collar workers have faced an increased risk of layoff or termination from the wave of large-firm restructuring in the U.S. economy. The increase in white-collar employment risk changes the relative demand for CBD accessibility, somewhat reducing the disparity between blue- and white-collar location demands that is attributable purely to employment risk differentness. These events by themselves lead to a weakening of the economic forces underlying spatial segregation of workers in the urban area by income level and employment sector.

Another point neglected in the text is how income risk affects estimates of the income elasticity of housing demand. When income risk is negatively correlated with income, as in the blue-/white-collar employment example cited previously, income elasticity estimates are biased upward. If, on the other hand, blue-collar workers in one urban area earn higher wages than blue-collar workers in a second urban area only as a compensating wage differential for working in an industry with greater risk of unemployment, then income elasticity estimates are biased downward. Thus, the income elasticity bias will vary depending upon the type of data used in the estimation.

There are reasons to expect income and housing price risks to be positively or negatively correlated in an urban area. Interpreting housing price as a user cost concept, the price includes expected capital gains or losses. One source of price risk is the uncertainty over capital gains or losses during the housing consumption period. It seems reasonable that capital gains are positively correlated with the regional business cycle; that is, because user cost rises as capital gains fall, housing price is negatively correlated with the regional business cycle. Workers who are employed in procyclical industries, therefore, have incomes that are likely negatively correlated with housing price, whereas workers who are employed in countercyclical industries have incomes that are positively correlated with housing price.

Turnbull et al. (1991) show that simultaneous income and price risks tend to provide reinforcing (offsetting) effects on housing and location demands when they are positively (negatively) correlated. These effects lead to more intricate patterns of spatial sorting of consumers within the urban area than in the certainty land-use models; workers in countercyclical industries will have lower housing demand and want to live closer to their jobs than otherwise identical workers in procyclical industries. The correlation between human capital and housing capital has identifiable effects on the housing and location demands of individuals in urban housing markets.

Turnbull's analysis has many results that should be examined empirically. Only then can we begin to move to the next level in understanding spatial consumer theory, and perhaps provide insights into the urban policies necessary for solving the problems of our cities.

# REFERENCES

Alonso, William. 1964. *Location and Land Use*. Cambridge, Mass.: Harvard University Press.

Anas, Alex. 1978. "Dynamics of Urban Growth." *Journal of Urban Economics* 5: 66–87.

Anas, Alex, and Ikki Kim. 1992. "Income Distribution and the Residential Density Gradient." *Journal of Urban Economics* 31: 164–80.

Andrulis, John. 1982. "Intra-Urban Workplace and Residential Mobility under Uncertainty." *Journal of Urban Economics* 11: 85–97.

Arrow, Kenneth J. 1970. *Essays in the Theory of Risk Bearing*. Chicago: Markham.

Bender, Bruce, and Hae-Shin Hwang. 1985. "Hedonic Housing Price Indices and Secondary Employment Centers." *Journal of Urban Economics* 17: 90–107.

Blackley, Dixie M., and James R. Follain. 1983. "Inflation, Tax Advantages to Homeownership, and the Locational Choices of Households." *Regional Science and Urban Economics* 13: 505–16.

————. 1987. "Tests of Locational Equilibrium in the Standard Urban Model." *Land Economics* 63: 46–61.

Block, M. K., and J. M. Heineke. 1973. "The Allocation of Effort under Uncertainty." *Journal of Political Economy* 81: 376–85.

Brown, Barbara. 1985. "Location and Housing Demand." *Journal of Urban Economics* 17: 30–41.

Brueckner, Jan K. 1980. "A Vintage Model of Urban Growth." *Journal of Urban Economics* 8: 389–402.

————. 1987. "The Structure of Urban Equilibria." In *The Handbook of Regional and Urban Economics, vol. 2*, edited by Edwin S. Mills (822–45). New York: Elsevier.

Brueckner, J. K., and D. Fansler. 1983. "The Economics of Urban Sprawl: Theory and Evidence on the Spatial Sizes of Cities." *Review of Economics and Statistics* 55: 479–82.

Capozza, Dennis, and Robert Helsley. 1989. "The Fundamentals of Land Prices and Urban Growth." *Journal of Urban Economics* 26: 295–306.

Carlton, Denise W., and Joseph Ferreira, Jr. 1977. "Selecting Subsidy Strategies for Housing Allowance Programs." *Journal of Urban Economics* 4: 221–47.

Cook, Paul. 1972. "A 'One Line' Proof of the Slutsky Equation." *American Economic Review* 62: 139.

Courant, P., and J. Yinger. 1977. "On Models of Racial Prejudice and Urban Residential Structure." *Journal of Urban Economics* 4: 272–91.

Cropper, Maureen L., and P. L. Gordon. 1991. "Wasteful Commuting: A Reexamination." *Journal of Urban Economics* 29: 2–13.

Dardanoni, Valintino. 1988. "Optimal Choices under Uncertainty." *Economic Journal* 98: 429–50.

Daughety, Andrew F. 1985. "Reconsidering Cournot: The Cournot Equilibrium is Consistent." *Rand Journal of Economics* 16: 368–79.

Davis, George K. 1989. "Income and Substitution Effects for Mean-Preserving Spreads." *International Economic Review* 30: 131–36.

deLeeuw, F. 1971. "The Demand for Housing—A Review of the Cross-Section Evidence." *Review of Economics and Statistics* 53: 1–10.

Deno, Kevin T., and Stephen L. Mehay. 1987. "Municipal Management Structure and Fiscal Performance: Do City Managers Make a Difference?" *Southern Economic Journal* 53: 627–42.

DeSalvo, Joseph S. 1977a. "Theory of Locally Employed Urban Household." *Journal of Regional Science* 17: 345–56.

————. 1977b. "Urban Household Behavior in a Model of Completely Centralized Employment." *Journal of Urban Economics* 17: 345–56.

————. 1985. "A Model of Urban Household Behavior with Leisure Choice." *Journal of Regional Science* 25: 159–74.

DeSalvo, Joseph S., and Louis R. Eeckhoudt. 1982. "Household Behavior under Income Uncertainty in a Monocentric Urban Area." *Journal of Urban Economics* 11: 99–111.

Dougan, William R., and Daphne A. Kenyon. 1988. "Pressure Groups and Expenditures: The Flypaper Effect Reconsidered." *Economic Inquiry* 26: 159–70.

Downs, Anthony. 1957. *An Economic Theory of Democracy.* New York: Harper & Row.

Eberts, Randall W. 1981. "An Empirical Investigation of Intraurban Wage Gradients." *Journal of Urban Economics* 10: 50–60.

Fischel, William A. 1990. *Do Growth Controls Matter?* Cambridge, Mass: Lincoln Institute of Land Policy.

Fisher, Ronald C. 1982. "Income and Grants Effects on Local Expenditure: The Flypaper Effect and Other Difficulties." *Journal of Urban Economics* 12: 324–45.

Follain, James R., and Steven Malpezzi. 1981. "The Flight to the Suburbs: Insights Gained from an Analysis of Central-City versus Suburban Housing Costs." *Journal of Urban Economics* 9: 381–98.

Frey, William H., and Elaine L. Fielding. 1994. "Changing Urban Populations: Regional Restructuring, Racial Polarization, and Poverty Concentrations." Population Studies Center, University of Michigan, Ann Arbor, February.

Fujita, Masahisa. 1982. "Spatial Patterns of Residential Development." *Journal of Urban Economics* 12: 22–52.

Galster, George C., and Sean P. Killen. 1994. "The Geography of Metropolitan Opportunity: A Reconnaissance and Conceptual Framework." Paper presented at 1994 Fannie Mae Conference, Washington, D.C.

Goodman, Allen C., and Masahiro Kawai. 1986. "Functional Form, Sample Selection, and Housing Demand." *Journal of Urban Economics* 20: 155–67.

Gramlich, Edward M., 1970. "The Effects of Federal Grants on State-Local Expenditures: A Review of the Econometric Literature." *1969 Proceedings of the Sixty-Second Annual Conference on Taxation.* Columbus, Ohio: National Tax Association.

Gramlich, Edward M., and David Rubinfeld. 1982. "Micro Estimates of Public Spending Demand Functions and Tests of the Tiebout and Median-Voter Hypotheses." *Journal of Political Economy* 90: 536–50.

Green, H. A. John. 1980. *Consumer Theory.* New York: Academic Press.

Hamilton, Bruce W. 1982. "Wasteful Commuting." *Journal of Political Economy* 90: 1035–53.

Hartwick, J., U. Schweizer, and P. Varaiya. 1976. "Comparative Statics of a Residential Economy with Several Classes." *Journal of Economic Theory* 13: 396–413.

Haurin, Donald R. 1981. "Local Income Taxation in an Urban Area." *Journal of Urban Economics* 10: 321–37.

Haurin, Donald R., and H. Leroy Gill. 1987. "Effects of Income Variability on the Demand for Owner-Occupied Housing." *Journal of Urban Economics* 22: 136–50.

Hekman, John S. 1980. "Income, Labor Supply, and Urban Residence." *American Economic Review* 70: 805–11.

Helsley, Robert W., and Arthur M. Sullivan. 1991. "Urban Subcenter Formation." *Regional Science and Urban Economics* 21: 255–75.

Henderson, J. Vernon. 1974. "The Sizes and Types of Cities." *American Economic Review* 64: 640–56.

————. 1982. "Systems of Cities in Closed and Open Economies." *Regional Science and Urban Economics* 12: 325–50.

Henderson, J. Vernon., and Y. M. Ioannides. 1983. "A Model of Housing Tenure Choice." *American Economic Review* 73: 98–113.

Herrin, William E., and Clifford R. Kern. 1992. "Testing the Standard Model of Residential Choice: An Implicit Markets Approach." *Journal of Urban Economics* 31: 145–63.

Hochman, Oded. 1982. "Congestable Local Public Goods in an Urban Setting." *Journal of Urban Economics* 11: 290–310.

Hochman, Oded, and David E. Pines. 1980. "Costs of Adjustment and Demolition Costs in Residential Construction and Their Effects on Urban Growth." *Journal of Urban Economics* 7: 2–19.

Holcombe, Randall G. 1980. "An Empirical Test of the Median Voter Model." *Economic Inquiry* 18: 260–74.

Holzer, Harry J. 1991. "The Spatial Mismatch Hypothesis: What Has the Evidence Shown?" *Urban Studies* 28: 105–22.

Ihlanfeldt, Keith R. 1992. "Intraurban Wage Gradients: Evidence by Race, Gender, Occupational Class, and Sector." *Journal of Urban Economics* 32: 70–91.

Inman, Robert P. 1978. "Testing the Political Economy's 'as if' Proposition: Is the Median Voter Really Decisive?" *Public Choice* 33: 45–65.

Kain, John F. 1987. "Computer Simulation Models of Urban Location." In *The Handbook of Regional and Urban Economics, vol. 2,* edited by Edwin S. Mills (848–75). New York: Elsevier.

Kern, C. 1981. "Racial Prejudice and Residential Segregation: The Yinger Model Revisited." *Journal of Urban Economics* 10: 164–73.

Leland, H. 1968. "Saving and Uncertainty: The Precautionary Demand for Saving." *Quarterly Journal of Economics* 82: 465–73.

Mankin, Wyatt. 1972. "A New Look at the Muth Model." *American Economic Review* 62: 980–81.

Mayo, Stephen K. 1981. "Theory and Estimation in the Economics of Housing Demand." *Journal of Urban Economics* 10: 95–116.

McEachern, Willian A. 1978. "Collective Decision Rules and Local Debt Choice: A Test of the Median Voter Hypothesis." *National Tax Journal* 31: 129–36.

McMillen, Daniel P., Ronald Jarmin, and Paul Thorsnes. 1992. "Selection Bias and Land Development in the Monocentric City Model." *Journal of Urban Economics* 31: 273–84.

Megdal, Sharon Bernstein. 1987. "The Flypaper Effect Revisited: An Econometric Explanation." *Review of Economics and Statistics* 59: 347–51.

Menezes, C. F., and D. L. Hanson. 1970. "On the Theory of Risk Aversion." *International Economic Review* 11: 481–87.

Mieszkowski, Peter, and Edwin S. Mills. 1993. "The Causes of Metropolitan Suburbanization." *Journal of Economic Perspectives* 7: 135–48.

Mills, Edwin S. 1967. "An Aggregate Model of Resource Allocation in a Metropolitan Area." *American Economic Review* 57: 197–210.

————. 1972. *Studies in the Structure of the Urban Economy.* Baltimore: Johns Hopkins University Press.

Mills, Edwin S., and Dennis de Ferranti. 1971. "Market Choices and Optimum City Size." *American Economic Review* 61: 340–45.

Miyao, Takahiro. 1975. "Dynamics and Comparative Statics in the Theory of Residential Location." *Journal of Economic Theory* 11: 113–46.

————. 1977. "A Long Run Analysis of Urban Growth Over Space." *Canadian Journal of Economics* 10: 678–86.

Mueller, Dennis C. 1989. *Public Choice II,* Cambridge, Mass.: Cambridge University Press.

Muth, Richard F. 1969. *Cities and Housing.* Chicago: University of Chicago Press.

————. 1985. "Models of Land Use, Housing, and Rent: An Evaluation." *Journal of Regional Science* 25: 593–606.

von Neumann, John, and Oscar Morgenstern. 1947. *Theory of Games and Economic Behavior,* 2d ed. New York: John Wiley & Sons.

Niskanen, Jr., William A. 1971. *Bureaucracy and Representative Government.* Chicago: Aldine-Atherton.

Oates, Wallace E. 1979. "Lump-Sum Intergovernmental Grants Have Price Effects." In *Fiscal Federalism and Grants-in-Aid,* edited by Peter Mieszkowski and Willian H. Oakland (23–29). Washington, D.C.: Urban Institute.

Ohls, J. C., and D. Pines. 1975. "Discontinuous Urban Development and Economic Efficiency." *Land Economics* 51: 224–34.

Papageorgiou, Yorgos Y. 1991. "Residential Choice When Place Utility Is Not Precisely Known in Advance." Working paper, McMaster University, Hamilton, Ontario. Photocopy.

Papageorgiou, Yorgos Y., and David Pines. 1988. "The Impact of Transportation Cost Uncertainty on Urban Structure." *Regional Science and Urban Economics* 18: 247–60.

Pasha, Hafiz A. 1992. "Comparative Statics Analysis of Density Controls." *Journal of Urban Economics* 32: 284–98.

Pines, David, and Efraim Sadka. 1986. "Comparative Statics of a Fully Closed City." *Journal of Urban Economics* 20: 1–20.

Polinsky, A. Mitchell, and David T. Ellwood. 1979. "An Empirical Reconciliation of Micro and Grouped Estimates of the Demand for Housing." *Review of Economics and Statistics* 61: 199–205.

Polinsky, A. M., and D. L. Rubinfeld. 1978. "The Long-Run Effects of a Residential Property Tax and Local Public Services." *Journal of Urban Economics* 5: 241–62.

Pratt, J. W. 1964. "Risk Aversion in the Small and in the Large." *Econometrica* 32: 122–36.

Rachlis, Mitchel B., and Anthony M. J. Yezer. 1985. "Urban Location and Housing Price Appreciation." *Papers of the Regional Science Association* 57: 156–64.

Romer, Thomas, and Howard Rosenthal. 1979a. "Bureaucrats versus Voters: On the Political Economy of Resource Allocation by Direct Democracy." *Quarterly Journal of Economics* 93: 563–88.

————. 1979b. "The Elusive Median Voter." *Journal of Public Economics* 12: 143–70.

————. 1980. "An Institutional Theory of the Effect of Intergovernmental Grants." *National Tax Journal* 33: 451–59.

————. 1982. "Median Voters or Budget Maximizers: Evidence from School District Referenda." *Economic Inquiry* 20: 556–78.

Rose-Ackerman, S. 1975. "Race and Urban Structure." *Journal of Urban Economics* 2: 85–103.

Sandmo, Agnar. 1970. "The Effect of Uncertainty on Savings Decisions." *Review of Economic Studies* 37: 353–60.

Sasaki, Komei. 1987. "A Comparative Static Analysis of Urban Structure in the Setting of Endogenous Income." *Journal of Urban Economics* 22: 53–72.

Small, Kenneth A., and Shunfeng Song. 1992. "'Wasteful' Commuting: A Resolution." *Journal of Political Economy* 100: 888–98.

Solow, R., and W. Vickery. 1971. "Land Use in a Long Narrow City." *Journal of Economic Theory* 3: 430–47.

Straszheim, Mahlon. 1984. "Urban Agglomeration Effects and Employment and Wage Gradients." *Journal of Urban Economics* 16: 187–207.

———. 1987. "The Theory of Urban Residential Location." In *The Handbook of Regional and Urban Economics, vol. 2*, edited by Edwin S. Mills (717–57). New York: Elsevier.

Sullivan, Arthur M. 1983. "A General Equilibrium Model with External Scale Economies in Production." *Journal of Urban Economics* 13: 235–55.

———. 1985. "The General-Equilibrium Effects of the Residential Property Tax: Incidence and Excess Burden." *Journal of Urban Economics* 18: 235–50.

Thurston, Lawrence, and Anthony M. J. Yezer. 1991. "Testing the Monocentric Urban Model: Evidence Based on Wasteful Commuting." *Journal of the American Real Estate and Urban Economics Association* 19: 41–51.

Turnbull, Geoffrey K. 1988a. "Market Structure, Location Rents, and the Land Development Process." *Journal of Urban Economics* 23: 261–77.

———. 1988b. "Residential Development in an Open City." *Regional Science and Urban Economics* 18: 307–20.

———. 1989. "Household Behavior in a Monocentric Urban Area with a Public Sector." *Journal of Urban Economics* 25: 103–15.

———. 1991. "The Spatial Demand for Housing with Uncertain Quality." *Journal of Real Estate Finance and Economics* 4: 1–14.

———. 1992a. "Fiscal Illusion, Uncertainty, and the Flypaper Effect." *Journal of Public Economics* 48: 207–23.

———. 1992b, "Location, Housing, and Leisure Demand under Local Employment." *Land Economics* 68: 62–71.

———. 1993a. "Housing Subsidies and Urban Household Behavior." *Journal of Regional Science* 34: 517–29.

———. 1993b. "Nonparametric Location Theory." *Journal of Real Estate Finance and Economics* 7: 169–84.

———. 1993c. "The Substitution Theorem in Urban Consumer Theory." *Journal of Urban Economics* 33: 331–43.

———. 1994. "Housing Demand Properties in the Monocentric Market Form." *Regional Science and Urban Economics* 24: 253–63.

Turnbull, Geoffrey K., and Salpie S. Djoundourian. 1994. "The Median Voter Hypothesis: Evidence from General Purpose Local Governments." *Public Choice* 81: 223–40.

Turnbull, Geoffrey K., John L. Glascock, and C. F. Sirmans. 1991. "Uncertain Income and Housing Price and Location Choice." *Journal of Regional Science* 31: 417–33.

Turnbull, Geoffrey K., and Yoshio Niho. 1986. "The Optimal Property Tax with Mobile Nonresidential Capital." *Journal of Public Economics* 29: 223–39.

Upton, C. 1981. "An Equilibrium Model of City Sizes." *Journal of Urban Economics* 10: 15–36.

Weiland, K. F. 1987. "An Extension of the Monocentric Urban Spatial Equilibrium Model to a Multicenter Setting: The Case of the Two Center City." *Journal of Urban Economics* 21: 259–71.

Wheaton, William C. 1974. "A Comparative Static Analysis of Urban Spatial Structure." *Journal of Economic Theory* 9: 223–37.

––––––. 1977a. "A Bid Rent Approach to Housing Demand." *Journal of Urban Economics* 4: 200–17.

––––––. 1977b. "Income and Urban Residence: An Analysis of Consumer Demand for Location." *American Economic Review* 67: 620–31.

––––––. 1982. "Urban Residential Growth under Perfect Foresight." *Journal of Urban Economics* 12: 1–21.

White, Michelle J. 1976. "Firm Suburbanization and Urban Subcenters." *Journal of Urban Economics* 3: 323–43.

––––––. 1978. "Job Suburbanization, Zoning, and the Welfare of Minority Groups." *Journal of Urban Economics* 5: 219–40.

––––––. 1988. "Urban Commuting Journeys are not 'Wasteful.'" *Journal of Political Economy* 96: 1097–1110.

Wildasin, David E. 1985. "Income Taxes and Urban Spatial Structure." *Journal of Urban Economics* 18: 313–33.

Wyckoff, Paul Gary. 1988. "A Bureaucratic Theory of Flypaper Effects." *Journal of Urban Economics* 23: 115–29.

Yamada, H. 1972. "On the Theory of Residential Location: Accessibility, Space, Leisure, and Environmental Quality." *Papers of the Regional Science Association* 29: 125–35.

Yinger, John. 1976. "Racial Prejudice and Racial Residential Segregation in an Urban Model." *Journal of Urban Economics* 3: 383–96.

––––––. 1979. "Prejudice and Discrimination in the Urban Housing Market." In *Current Issues in Urban Economics*, edited by Peter Mieszkowski and Mahlon Straszheim. Baltimore, Md.: Johns Hopkins University Press.

_____. 1992a. "An Analysis of the Efficiency of Urban Residential Structure, with an Application to Racial Integration." *Journal of Urban Economics* 31: 388–407.

_____. 1992b. "City and Suburb: Urban Models with More than One Employment Center." *Journal of Urban Economics* 31: 181–205.

# ABOUT THE AUTHOR

**Geoffrey K. Turnbull** is the C. J. Brown Distinguished Professor of Real Estate in the Department of Economics, Louisiana State University. He is a member of the editorial boards for the *Journal of Urban Economics*, *Journal of Real Estate Economics and Finance*, and *Real Estate Economics*. In addition to location theory, his research focuses on the urban land development process and local public finance.

# ABOUT THE COMMENTATORS

**James R. Follain** is a professor of economics and senior research associate in the Center for Policy Research of the Maxwell School of Citizenship and Public Affairs at Syracuse University. His research examines a wide variety of topics in real estate economics and finance, urban and regional economics, taxation, and financial institutions. He has produced over 50 publications for many different audiences.

**C. F. Sirmans,** professor of finance and real estate and director of the Center for Real Estate and Urban Economic Studies, University of Connecticut, specializes in the analysis of real estate. He has written, lectured, and consulted extensively on a wide range of real estate topics, including real estate investments, mortgages, lease valuation, and housing. He is the author of six textbooks on real estate and has published over 100 articles in a variety of real estate, finance and economics journals.

# ABOUT THE INSTITUTIONS

**THE AMERICAN REAL ESTATE AND URBAN ECONOMICS AS-SOCIATION (AREUEA)** was organized at the 1964 meeting of the Allied Social Science Associations in Chicago. AREUEA grew from the discussions of individuals who recogized a need for more information and analysis in the fields of real estate development, planning, and economics. Events since that time have more than justified the concerns felt by the founders of AREUEA. The continuing efforts of the association have advanced the scope of knowledge in these disciplines, and have facilitated the exchange of information and opinions among academic, professional, and governmental people who are concerned with urban economics and real estate issues.

Specifically, the purposes of AREUEA are to promote education and encourage research in real estate, urban economics, and related areas; to improve communication and exchange of information in real estate, urban economics, and allied areas among college and university faculty members; and to facilitate the association of academic, practicing professional, and research persons in real estate, urban economics, and allied areas.

**THE URBAN INSTITUTE** is a nonprofit research and educational organization established in Washington, D.C., in 1968. Its staff investigates the social and economic problems confronting the nation and public and private means to alleviate them. The Urban Institute has three goals for its research and dissemination activities: to sharpen thinking about societal problems and efforts to solve them, to improve government decisions and performance, and to increase citizen awareness of important public choices.

Through work that ranges from broad conceptual studies to administrative and technical assistance, Institute researchers contribute to the stock of knowledge and the analytic tools available to guide decision-making in the public interest.

The Institute disseminates its research and the research of others through the publications program of its Press.

The American Real Estate And Urban Economics Association (ARE-UEA) was organized in 1964 based on the perceived need to improve information and analysis in the fields of real estate development, planning, and urban economics. The AREUEA Monograph Series is designed to provide teachers, students, and practitioners with a comprehensive and timely presentation of recent research materials translated into summary form, which is more quickly and easily comprehended than journal articles and specialized studies. These monographs review old views, new techniques, and recent data. They should be particularly useful as supplements to classroom instruction or continuing professional education of practitioners.

Development of the AREUEA Monographs is supervised by a committee appointed by the AREUEA Board of Directors. In order to ensure balanced coverage, outside commentators are invited to provide suggestions for revision to the author and to add brief comments on elements of the literature which supplement the body of the monograph. For this second monograph, James R. Follain and C. F. Sirmans have each provided a commentary.

The AREUEA Monograph Committee:
Anthony M.J. Yezer, Series Editor
George Washington University

Patric H. Hendershott
Ohio State University

David Ling
University of Florida

James D. Shilling
University of Wisconsin

# INDEX